Tech Ambassadors

Bridging Governments And Silicon Valley

Hichem Karoui

Global East-West (London)

Copyright © [2024] by Hichem Karoui

"Sociology and Sociologists": A Global East-West Series

All rights reserved.

No portion of this book may be reproduced without written permission from the publisher or author except as permitted by copyright law.

Contents

1. Introduction: The Rise of Techplomacy — 1
2. The Role of Tech Ambassadors in Modern Diplomacy — 25
3. Tech Giants as Geopolitical Actors — 43
4. Navigating Issues of State Sovereignty in the Digital Age — 57
5. Impact of Social Media on International Relations — 75
6. Cybersecurity and the Intersection of Tech and Policy — 95
7. Emerging Technologies: AI, Quantum Computing, and Biotechnology — 115
8. The Technological Arms Race and Global Power Dynamics — 135
9. Ethical Responsibilities of Tech Companies in Global Affairs — 159
10. Establishing Global Regulatory Frameworks for Emerging Technologies — 175

11. Technological Sovereignty and National Security	193
12. The Future of Techplomacy: Challenges and Opportunities	213
Bibliography	235

1

Introduction: The Rise of Techplomacy

Defining Techplomacy

IN THE LABYRINTHINE INTERSECTION of silicon and statecraft, Techplomacy emerges as a fascinating chimera - part digital revolution, part age-old diplomatic dance. This metamorphosis of traditional diplomacy doesn't merely represent an evolutionary step; rather, it heralds a seismic shift in how nations navigate the treacherous waters of international relations amid the digital tempest.

Like a complex algorithmic dance, Techplomacy weaves through the fabric of modern governance, where lines of code carry as much weight as lines in treaties. In this brave new world, where bits and bytes traverse borders at light speed, the traditional ambassadorial briefcase has been replaced by encrypted drives and digital signatures. The diplomatic corps now wrestles with artificial intelligence, cryptocurrency regulations, and cyber sovereignty alongside their traditional concerns about territorial integrity and trade relations (Mario Torres Jarrín and Riordan, 2023).

The historical trajectory from sealed wax to secured servers tells a compelling tale of diplomatic evolution. Where once diplomats exchanged carefully worded missives via mounted couriers, they now navigate virtual corridors of power, their influence extending through fiber-optic cables and satellite links. This transformation hasn't simply accelerated communication; it has fundamentally restructured the architecture of international dialogue, creating new pressure points and possibilities in the global chess game.

The fingerprints of Techplomacy are increasingly visible on the face of international affairs - from state-sponsored hackers probing digital defenses to social media campaigns swaying electoral outcomes across continents. These digital dynamics have birthed new forms of statecraft, where a well-timed tweet might carry the diplomatic weight of a formal démarche and where cyber capabilities can shift the balance of power as decisively as traditional military might. In this rapidly evolving landscape, mastery of digital diplomacy has become as crucial as command of traditional diplomatic protocols.

- Techplomacy refers to the integration of technology into diplomatic practices, where technology companies are treated as geopolitical actors. This shift is driven by the increasing role of technology in geopolitical confrontations and the need for governments to engage with tech companies on issues like data sovereignty and cybersecurity(Jarrín & Riordan, 2023).

- Denmark pioneered this approach by appointing a Tech Ambassador in 2017, highlighting the importance of technology in foreign policy. This initiative aims to bridge the gap between traditional diplomacy and the tech industry, addressing the diplomatic deficit created by rapid technological advancements("Diplomacy in the Digital Age: Lessons from Denmark's TechPlomacy Initiative", 2022) (Klynge et al., 2020).

Key players in the Techplomacy field include diverse stakeholders such as governments, major technology companies, international organizations, and non-state actors. These entities play a significant role in developing and implementing Techplomatic strategies, shaping the framework of global political interactions. Strategic technology ambassadors emerge as essential figures, facilitating dialogue, negotiation, and collaboration among different parties.(Corneliu Bjola and Zaiotti 2020)

However, the rapid rise of technological changes presents significant challenges to established diplomatic practices. Social media's ability to spread misinformation quickly, along with cyber threats to national security, demands innovative strategies for Techplomatic engagement. While these disruptions present difficulties, they also open up opportunities for creative solutions and strong collaborations in the Techplomacy landscape. Successfully navigating these challenges and opportunities is essential for fostering a sustainable future in Techplomacy. (Mario Torres Jarrín and Riordan 2023)

Different nations have exhibited varying degrees of adaptability and foresight in response to the relentless pace of digitalization. Some have embraced technological changes through proactive policies, while others struggle with the destabilizing effects of these disruptions. This array of responses highlights the need for a sophisticated understanding of global digitalization trends within the scope of Techplomacy. Anticipating future developments in Techplomacy requires a careful analysis of ongoing shifts in global power structures, emerging technologies, and geopolitical changes. Understanding how Techplomatic efforts may evolve provides invaluable insights for policymakers, diplomats, and technologists, enabling them to navigate the complexities of international relations and digital advancements.

Historical Context: The Evolution of Diplomacy

Diplomacy first breathed life in the shadows of ancient courts and marble halls through wandering emissaries who carried whispered promises between realms. These early diplomatic dancers—sometimes revered, occasionally poisoned—wove delicate webs of peace through carefully chosen words and symbolic gestures, their success measured in bloodless resolutions rather than battlefield victories.

The birth of nation-states unleashed an unprecedented diplomatic revolution: Permanent embassies sprouted like stone gardens in foreign capitals, while ambassadors—those elegant spies wrapped in diplomatic immunity—crafted intricate networks of influence through lavish balls and clandestine meetings. Imagine the transformative chaos when steam-powered ships and telegraph wires suddenly collapsed vast distances, forcing diplomatic practices to evolve at breakneck speed or risk irrelevance in an increasingly interconnected world.

The 20th century's diplomatic landscape exploded into dazzling complexity. While the smoking ruins of two world wars still smoldered, multilateral diplomacy emerged phoenix-like through the United Nations' creation - a grand experiment in global governance that forever altered how nations spoke to one another. Yet it was the Cold War's end that truly shattered traditional diplomatic boundaries, as economic interests began conducting their own shadow diplomacy through boardrooms and trade agreements.

Now, in our hyper-connected age, diplomacy shape-shifts once again. Traditional handshakes and sealed documents dance alongside viral tweets and virtual summits, while ambassadors navigate both physical embassies and digital battlegrounds. This technological metamorphosis hasn't merely changed how diplomacy functions - it's fundamentally transformed what diplomacy means in a world where power flows through fiber optic cables as readily as it once did through royal proclamations.

Convergence of Technology and Diplomacy

The confluence of technology and diplomacy ushers in a profound metamorphosis—an era where the age-old rituals of international relations collide and coalesce with the ceaseless pulse of technological innovation. This fusion disrupts entrenched paradigms, dismantles spatial and temporal constraints, and redefines the lexicon of global engagement. At its core lies a duality: the boundless potential of connectivity and the labyrinthine challenges it summons, demanding both dexterity and foresight from those navigating this shifting landscape.

Central to this transformation is the advent of digital communication, a force that compresses distance and obliterates the inertia of geography. In virtual realms, dialogue unfolds in real time—elastic, instantaneous, and unconstrained. The tactile choreography once demanded by physical summits now finds a spectral counterpart in virtual conferences and transcontinental teleconferences, where the immediacy of engagement propels diplomatic agendas with unprecedented velocity. Decisions that once simmered over days now erupt into fruition in hours, a testament to the speed at which global leaders convene across digital domains. (Wilson Dizard Jr 2001)

Parallel to this dynamic immediacy is the embrace of data-driven diplomacy—a paradigm where raw information transcends its passive state, becoming an active instrument in the diplomatic arsenal. Vast torrents of data are sifted, parsed, and molded into strategic insight, enabling nations to decode the sentiments of global populations, anticipate ruptures in geopolitical equilibrium, and craft strategies forged from analytical precision. Predictive analytics serve as a modern oracle, charting the possible futures of international landscapes and equipping decision-makers with the agility to maneuver amidst the shifting tides of global affairs. Yet within this data deluge lies a silent caveat: the risks of over-reliance on statistical models and the ethical quagmires posed by their deployment. (Wilson Dizard Jr 2001)

Simultaneously, the rise of connectivity has injected new vigor—and volatility—into the realm of public diplomacy. Social media platforms, digital campaigns, and virtual narratives have armed nations with potent tools to engage the collective consciousness of global audiences, offering mechanisms to project ideologies, cultivate alliances, and weave their cultural identity into the tapestry of international influence. Yet, the transparency of this ecosystem cuts both ways. Misinformation metastasizes like radioactive decay, cyber vulnerabilities threaten to dismantle public trust, and the unrelenting feedback loops of digital opinion demand deft and rapid responses. Herein, soft power becomes not a steady stream but a fluid exchange animated by likes, shares, and the fragmented truths of the information age.

Amid this maelstrom of interconnectivity lies a darker frontier—cyber-diplomacy, a domain fraught with ethical dilemmas and existential stakes. Espionage has transcended physical boundaries, morphing into shadowy incursions through strings of code, while cyberattacks conflate virtual and geopolitical sovereignty, destabilizing nations without crossing a single physical border. The militarization of cyberspace demands that diplomacy become as much a bulwark as a bridge, necessitating intricate strategies to safeguard digital architectures, subdue clandestine threats, and negotiate the precarious interplay of power and vulnerability.

The intertwining of technology and diplomacy illuminates a narrative imbued with potential and peril. It implores nations, diplomats, and thought leaders to adopt not merely pragmatic action but a visionary ethos that comprehends the rhythms of technological progress without succumbing to their unchecked acceleration. In an ever-complex nexus of opportunity and consequence, diplomacy must evolve—not as the passive recipient of technological influence but as its active navigator, shaping the contour of a digital world unbound.

Notable Case Studies in Techplomacy

The intersection of technology and diplomacy presents a rich tapestry of case studies that highlight the evolving dynamics and challenges of techplomacy. Prominent among these is the technological rivalry between the United States and China, a multifaceted competition that spans geopolitical arenas, economic policies, and technological advancements. This rivalry centers on disputes over intellectual property, the global race for 5G dominance, and broader cybersecurity issues. Together, these tensions underscore how technological supremacy has become a critical axis in shaping modern international relations.

Equally compelling is the realm of cybersecurity and its implications for statecraft. The Stuxnet attack on Iran's nuclear facilities stands as a landmark in digital hostilities, illustrating not just the destructive potential of cyber tools but their sweeping implications for modern diplomacy. Subsequent cyberattacks launched by nation-states have revealed the murkiness of attribution and the challenges of establishing accountability, thereby amplifying calls for international cooperation. These incidents emphasize the urgency of fostering diplomatic frameworks aimed at addressing the destabilizing nature of cyber conflict and reducing the pervasive risks of a borderless, interconnected digital domain. (Meryem Marzouki and Calderaro 2022)

The European Union's General Data Protection Regulation (GDPR) also emerges as a defining example of techplomacy. By safeguarding personal data and setting robust standards for data protection, the GDPR has reshaped global discourse on digital governance. Its influence extends far beyond Europe, compelling countries around the globe to revisit their data policies and recalibrate their legislative priorities. This case reflects how regulatory frameworks, born of diplomatic efforts, can establish normative benchmarks that shape international technological ecosystems and recalibrate the rules of engagement for global actors. (Corneliu Bjola and Zaiotti 2020)

Technology companies, too, have become pivotal actors in the techplomacy landscape. The controversies surrounding social media platforms, particularly concerning allegations of election interference and the proliferation of misinformation, have blurred the lines between state and corporate responsibility. These incidents have prompted intensified scrutiny over tech companies' accountability, illuminating their dual role as enablers of global connectivity and potential disruptors of democratic processes. This juncture has triggered policy discussions between governments and corporations, forcing the redefinition of governance structures that address private sector participation within the diplomatic sphere. (Corneliu Bjola and Zaiotti 2020)

Finally, the frontier of emerging technologies—particularly artificial intelligence and biotechnology—represents an evolving and high-stakes case study in techplomacy. With these innovations poised to transform societies, economies, and warfare, nations face the dual challenges of leveraging their benefits while mitigating their risks. The international quest to develop norms, ethical standards, and regulatory mechanisms for these technologies reflects the painstaking process of achieving consensus in an arena defined by rapid innovation and competing interests. From setting guardrails for AI to addressing bioethics in genetic engineering, these negotiations exemplify the complexities of fostering shared responsibility within the global technological landscape.

Altogether, these case studies reveal the multilayered nature of techplomacy. They offer a lens into how technology and diplomacy converge, conflict, and coalesce to shape an interconnected and digitally driven world order. Through competition, collaboration, and innovation, techplomacy continues to redefine the boundaries of international relations in the 21st century.

Key Players in the Techplomacy Landscape

Techplomacy represents an intricate web of strategic interactions, where the seismic interplay between technology and global diplomacy reshuffles traditional hierarchies of power and influence. In this shifting paradigm, a triad of dominant actors—governments, multinational corporations, and non-governmental organizations (NGOs)—emerges, each wielding distinct yet interconnected clout over the constantly evolving nexus of technology and international relations.

Governments, as architects of regulatory framings and geopolitical strategy, remain pivotal in Techplomacy's sprawling arena. Their efforts encompass everything from enshrining domestic digital policies to addressing transnational technological threats with nuanced diplomacy. The United States and China, locked in a high-stakes rivalry over artificial intelligence and semiconductor supremacy, exemplify the geopolitical heft of state actors, while European Union nations strive to propagate comprehensive regulatory frameworks like the GDPR, setting benchmarks for global digital governance. Policy interventions, whether through strategic alliances or retaliatory measures such as sanctions on technology exports, underscore the assertive, nation-driven dimensions of diplomacy in the digital age. (Meryem Marzouki and Calderaro 2022)

However, multinational corporations increasingly blur the boundaries of sovereignty and influence, commanding not just vast economic resources but profound authority in shaping technological norms. Giants such as Google, Apple, Facebook, and Amazon—often dubbed the "Big Tech oligarchs"—operate as quasi-diplomatic entities, engaging directly with governments and international bodies while establishing soft power over global information flows, data privacy frameworks, and infrastructural innovation. Their lobbying efforts and cross-border operations magnify their entanglement in global policy-making, rendering these profit-driven entities de facto architects of aspects of global order, in some cases outpacing formal diplomatic protocols.

- Major technology companies such as Google and Alibaba have emerged as influential players, affecting trade dynamics and national policies. Their global reach and impact on digital economies necessitate diplomatic engagement(Farman-Farmaian & Pir-Budagyan, 2023).

- Denmark's Tech Ambassador initiative represents a new form of coalition building, engaging industry, governments, and institutions to address the opportunities and risks posed by technology("Diplomacy in the Digital Age: Lessons from Denmark's TechPlomacy Initiative", 2022) (Klynge et al., 2020).

Meanwhile, non-governmental organizations assert their voice in this dynamic interplay, focusing on critical advocacy areas such as digital rights, cybersecurity, and ethical applications of emerging technologies. NGOs like Access Now and the Electronic Frontier Foundation challenge state and corporate overreach, lobbying for human-centered governance while amplifying the rights of marginalized groups in the digital sphere. By positioning themselves as watchdogs of liberty and privacy, they act as counterweights to both governmental and corporate overreach, introducing a moral vector into what might otherwise be coldly calculated spheres of Techplomacy.

These deeply interwoven interactions illustrate the multi-stakeholder nature of Techplomacy—a jigsaw where statecraft, economics, and ethics are constantly reconfigured through collaborations and confrontations. International diplomacy no longer resides solely in the corridors of embassies but unfolds in cyberspace, boardrooms, and activist forums, underscoring the necessity of recalibrating our understanding of power in this technologically mediated world. Ultimately, as everything from global security to digital freedoms hinges on this labyrinthine structure, comprehending the intricacies of Techplomacy is not merely an academic exercise but a practical imperative for navigating 21st-century international relations.

The Strategic Significance of Technology Ambassadors

In today's interconnected world, the emergence of technology ambassadors has become crucial in shaping international relations and diplomatic strategies. These representatives extend beyond mere affiliation with their respective technology companies; they function as key influencers within the intricate framework of foreign policy and geopolitical strategy. The importance of technology ambassadors lies in their unique ability to connect technological innovation with diplomatic engagement, acting as intermediaries who navigate the complexities of digital advancement and global governance.(Meryem Marzouki and Calderaro 2022)

Technology ambassadors play a significant role in promoting the interests and initiatives of their organizations on a global scale. They articulate their companies' visions and values, aligning them with national and international diplomatic objectives. By fostering meaningful dialogues and encouraging collaborations, these ambassadors facilitate the exchange of innovative ideas and best practices, which contributes to the integration of technological advancements into the global diplomatic discourse.

Moreover, the role of technology ambassadors extends beyond corporate representation. They offer essential insights to policymakers regarding the implications of new technologies across various socio-political contexts. Whether dealing with issues of data privacy, cybersecurity complexities, or ethical challenges posed by artificial intelligence, technology ambassadors provide nuanced perspectives that enrich diplomatic discussions and inform policy development.(Meryem Marzouki and Calderaro 2022)

Additionally, these ambassadors advocate for the responsible use of technology globally. Through strategic interactions with government officials, industry leaders, and civil society organizations, they advance initiatives designed to strengthen ethical standards and regulatory frameworks governing the deployment of emerging technologies. Their influence in shaping public dialogue and garnering support for ethical guidelines highlights their essential role in directing the course of tech-related international relations.

Technological Disruptions and Their Diplomatic Consequences

The relentless acceleration of technological innovation has catalyzed seismic shifts across commerce, communication, and governance, jolting the global arena into uncharted terrains. These disruptions, far from being contained, have infiltrated the intricate web of international relations, presenting a mosaic of challenges and unprecedented opportunities for diplomacy. Among the most significant upheavals is the meteoric rise of digital currencies and blockchain technology, which now dominate financial debates worldwide. Cryptocurrencies, infamous for their volatility and decentralization, have upended traditional financial orthodoxies, forcing nations to grapple with intricate dilemmas surrounding monetary policy, cross-border transactions, and the sovereignty of economic frameworks. The challenge for global leaders lies in engineering cooperative frameworks that embrace innovation's promise while erecting safeguards to ward against instability. Diplomatic maneuvers must thread the needle between enabling digital financial evolution and anchoring global financial security within a prudent yet progressive regulatory scaffold.

Equally transformative has been the advent of social media and instant messaging applications, a paradigm shift that has irreversibly altered the mechanisms of public diplomacy. Platforms once associated solely with personal communication have metamorphosed into geopolitical battlegrounds, offering instantaneous, borderless influence over public sentiment and socio-political discourse. Governments now grapple with the dual-edged nature of these digital conduits—balancing the potential for narrative control and outreach with the threats posed by misinformation and malign foreign influence. Strategic digital engagement has become indispensable, transcending traditional diplomatic practice to apprehend the enigmatic sphere of global audiences with precision and foresight. (Meryem Marzouki and Calderaro 2022)

Simultaneously, AI and automation technologies have unraveled the threads of conventional labor paradigms, sparking existential debates about the future of work and societal equity. By displacing traditional industries and redefining skill demands, the AI revolution demands urgent international discourse to harmonize technological momentum with inclusivity. At this juncture, diplomacy assumes a central role—not merely to guide the ethical governance of AI but to foster a global commons in which technology advances without sidelining human integrity, data trustworthiness, or fairness in automated decisions. Multilateral agreements on AI ethics, transparency, and accountability form an essential bulwark against dystopian outcomes in the face of such seismic shifts.

Yet, the technological transformation narrative darkens further with the looming specter of cybersecurity frailties and the militarization of emerging technologies. The fragility of interconnected digital systems poses existential risks, from the weaponization of AI to cyberattacks targeting critical infrastructure. These omnipresent threats expose the fault lines in global security systems, demanding cohesive action to construct defensive architectures capable of withstanding adversaries' ever-evolving tactics. Establishing robust cyber defense alliances, promoting symmetrical information exchange, and drafting globally enforceable cybersecurity treaties are not mere aspirations—they are imperatives of our connected age. (Meryem Marzouki and Calderaro 2022)

This technological upheaval, sprawling and unrelenting, amplifies the urgency for nuanced, anticipatory diplomacy. Future-ready policies must internalize the intricate tapestry of technological disruptions while embracing flexibility to adapt in real time. In this volatile digital epoch, the craft of diplomacy stands not as a relic of tradition but as the linchpin to coordinated, harmonious progress. Only by fostering multilateral dialogue, actionable cooperation, and an unflagging commitment to ethical stewardship can nations chart a course through this unparalleled transformation of the global order.

Challenges and Opportunities in Techplomacy

The expanding landscape of Techplomacy undeniably melds technological innovation with intricate geopolitical realities, reshaping international relations in both transformative and contentious ways. Chief among the challenges is the inherent lag between the swift proliferation of disruptive technologies and the strained efforts of global governance frameworks to catch up. This misalignment fosters contested zones, where emerging domains like artificial intelligence, biotechnology, and quantum computing lack universally agreed-upon norms and regulations. The absence of such frameworks exacerbates vulnerabilities—cybersecurity breaches, intellectual property theft, and unilateral exploitation of technology standards—stoking geopolitical rivalries. For instance, the US-China tech rivalry exemplifies how technological dominance becomes a lever for both economic supremacy and security strategy, intensifying tensions in global trade and supply chains (Bjola & Zaiotti, 2020).

The cybersecurity domain further illuminates the precarious interplay of Techplomacy. High-profile incidents like the Stuxnet cyberattack underline the destabilizing potential of state-sponsored cyber operations in undermining trust and challenging traditional notions of sovereignty (Dizard Jr., 2001). Technology firms themselves are thrust into this evolving nexus as quasi-sovereign actors, wielding outsized influence on sensitive issues like data governance and misinformation control. While the EU's GDPR demonstrates progress in ensuring data protection and privacy, it also reveals the fragmented nature of tech regulation: disparate policies across nations often impede cohesive global strategies (Marzouki & Calderaro, 2022). This landscape increasingly necessitates public-private partnerships, as states alone are ill-equipped to address the multi-layered challenges of hybrid threats—where misinformation campaigns, cyberattacks, and traditional diplomacy intertwine.

Yet, embedded within these challenges are profound opportunities. Advances in technology afford a renewed impetus for multilateral cooperation, particularly in shared global priorities like combating climate change or mitigating pandemics through healthcare innovation. For example, technological tools enabling real-time environmental monitoring or rapid vaccine rollouts create platforms for trust-building among nations. Furthermore, Techplomacy can spearhead efforts to bridge the global digital divide, fostering equity through initiatives that prioritize access to digital infrastructure and skills, particularly in the Global South. Such endeavors not only bolster economic development but also amplify soft power, strengthening the legitimacy of diplomatic alliances.

Simultaneously, technology has revolutionized diplomacy itself. Digital tools have rendered diplomacy more accessible and immediate, with platforms like Twitter transforming traditional statecraft into dynamic, multidirectional dialogues. This democratization of communication empowers non-state actors and civil society to engage directly with and influence international policy discussions. However, it also places greater responsibility on states and tech companies to navigate these platforms responsibly, countering malign uses while enhancing public trust.

Ultimately, Techplomacy operates within a paradox: while it extends pathways for collaboration and innovation, it sharpens the stakes of competition and conflict. Addressing this duality requires both imaginative foresight and agile adaptation—blending geopolitical strategy with technological expertise to forge a resilient, inclusive, and cooperative digital future.

- The convergence of technology and diplomacy presents challenges such as cyber warfare, disinformation, and ethical concerns related to AI and surveillance. These issues require international collaboration and new diplomatic norms(Farman-Farmaian & Pir-Budagyan, 2023).

- On the positive side, technology offers tools for enhanced communication, cultural exchange, and solutions to global challenges like climate change and public health. Digital diplomacy has become integral to diplomatic tasks, including negotiations and information sharing(Eggeling, 2023) (Farman-Farmaian & Pir-Budagyan, 2023).

As the dynamics of Techplomacy continue to evolve, there is a pressing need to seize these opportunities while effectively addressing the accompanying challenges. Navigating the complexities inherent in technology-driven diplomacy requires foresight and strategic insight to steer global affairs toward a more stable and inclusive future. By leveraging the transformative potential of

Techplomacy, stakeholders can foster resilient and cooperative international relations, laying a foundation for sustainable progress and innovation in an interconnected world.

Global Responses to Digitalization

Drawing from the provided context and references, I'll revise and enhance the text while maintaining its core message about digital transformation and international relations:

The digital revolution has catalyzed an unprecedented era of global metamorphosis, characterized by intricate webs of connectivity and technological advancement that fundamentally reshape human interaction and governance structures. This transformation transcends traditional boundaries, compelling nations to navigate an increasingly complex digital ecosystem while balancing domestic imperatives with international obligations.

At the forefront of this evolution is the strategic development of comprehensive digital frameworks. Governments worldwide are orchestrating ambitious digital agendas that encompass everything from foundational infrastructure development to advanced technological integration. These initiatives reflect a sophisticated understanding of the multifaceted nature of digital transformation, incorporating elements of social inclusion, economic innovation, and technological sovereignty (Mario Torres Jarrín and Riordan, 2023).

The digital landscape has emerged as a critical diplomatic battleground, where traditional geopolitical tensions intersect with novel technological challenges. Nations must navigate this terrain while addressing fundamental questions of digital sovereignty, data governance, and cybersecurity. The resulting diplomatic framework, termed "Techplomacy," represents a fusion of technological expertise and diplomatic finesse, essential for managing the complexities of modern international relations (Wilson Dizard Jr, 2001).

This digital transformation has precipitated a fundamental shift in how nations perceive and protect their strategic interests. The emergence of cyber threats has elevated digital security to a national security imperative, prompting governments to develop sophisticated defensive and offensive capabilities. Simultaneously, the need for international cooperation has never been more acute, as digital challenges increasingly transcend national boundaries and require coordinated responses (Meryem Marzouki and Calderaro, 2022).

The global community now stands at a crucial juncture where the decisions made about digital governance will profoundly influence the future of international relations. Success in this new era demands a delicate balance between national interests and global cooperation, technological advancement and ethical considerations, security concerns, and open innovation.

Future Directions for Techplomacy

As society stands at the crossroads of technological advances and diplomatic engagement, it becomes clear that Techplomacy will be essential in shaping global dynamics. The ongoing integration of advanced technologies into societal structures calls for a proactive and strategically sophisticated approach to diplomacy. Potential future paths for Techplomacy focus on several key considerations.

The rapid evolution of transformative technologies demands a robust framework of international governance. Through Techplomacy, nations can forge vital partnerships that transcend traditional diplomatic boundaries, creating shared protocols for ethical innovation. These frameworks must balance technological advancement with human welfare, establishing clear guidelines for AI development, quantum research, and biotechnology applications. By fostering multilateral dialogue, we can develop comprehensive standards that promote responsible innovation while protecting against potential misuse. This collaborative approach enables nations to harness emerging technologies' benefits while maintaining stringent safeguards against unintended consequences. Such diplomatic efforts must prioritize transparency, equitable access, and sustainable development, ensuring that technological progress serves global interests rather than exacerbating existing disparities. The establishment of these norms requires ongoing engagement, adaptive governance structures, and commitment to shared ethical principles that reflect our collective aspirations for a technologically advanced yet responsible future.

The future of Techplomacy will also be closely linked to the concept of digital sovereignty. As countries seek to protect their digital infrastructures and data security, tensions between technological innovation and national security may increase. Effective Techplomacy must address these intricate dynamics by endorsing collaborative strategies that respect both technological development and national interests. This approach requires a delicate balance between encouraging innovation and preserving sovereignty, calling for savvy diplomatic maneuvers that build mutual trust and cooperation.

Moreover, the role of technology ambassadors is likely to evolve alongside the growing influence of technology in global affairs. These representatives will need to possess technological expertise and a deep understanding of geopolitical nuances and cross-cultural dynamics. Future directions for Techplomacy will emphasize cultivating a new generation of diplomats skilled at navigating the complex interactions between technological progress and diplomatic relations, effectively bridging the gap between innovation and governance.

Looking ahead, Techplomacy is destined to become a crucial tool for mediating cyber conflicts and promoting cyber resilience. The increase in harmful cyber activities underscores the need for collaborative responses that transcend national boundaries. Future initiatives in Techplomacy may focus on establishing robust networks for information sharing, joint cybersecurity efforts, and capacity-building initiatives to enhance collective defense against cyber threats. Such efforts will require a unified commitment from the international community, reflecting the interdependent nature of cybersecurity in a digitized world.

In conclusion, the future pathways for Techplomacy signal a transformational shift in diplomatic practices, embodying the intricate fusion of technological innovation and international relations. Embracing these paths necessitates strategic thinking, innovative frameworks, and adaptable diplomacy in line with rapid technological change. As society navigates this evolving landscape, recognizing the multifaceted dimensions of Techplomacy will be vital in fostering a more secure, equitable, and cooperative global environment.

References

- Bjola, Corneliu, and Ruben Zaiotti. Digital Diplomacy and International Organisations. Routledge, 2020.

- Casper, Klynge, Mikael Ekman, and Nikolaj Juncher Waedegaard. "Chapter 12: Diplomacy in the Digital Age: Lessons from Denmark's TechPlomacy Initiative." In Ministries of Foreign Affairs in the World, 263–272. 2022. DOI: https://doi.org/10.1163/9789004505889_013.

- Casper, Klynge, Mikael Ekman, and Nikolaj Juncher Waedegaard. "Diplomacy in the Digital Age: Lessons from Denmark's TechPlomacy Initiative." The Hague Journal of Diplomacy 15, no. 2 (2020). DOI: 10.1163/1871191X-15101094.

- Daria, Farman-Farmaian, and Mikael Pir-Budagyan. "The Interplay of Technology and International Relations: A Historical and Forward-Looking Perspective." Georgetown Journal of International Affairs (2023). DOI: 10.1353/gia.2023.a913637.

- Eggeling, Kristin Anabel. "Digital Diplomacy." Oxford Research Encyclopedia of International Studies (2023). DOI: 10.1093/acrefore/9780190846626.013.790.

- Jarrín, Mario Torres, and Shaun Riordan. Science Diplomacy, Cyberdiplomacy and Techplomacy in EU-LAC Relations. Springer Nature, 2023.

- Jarrín, Mario Torres, and Shaun Riordan. "Techplomacy." In United Nations University Series on Regionalism. 2023. DOI: 10.1007/978-3-031-36868-4_5.

- Marzouki, Meryem, and Andrea Calderaro. Internet Diplomacy. Rowman & Littlefield, 2022.

- Wilkerson, Dizard Jr. Wilson. Digital Diplomacy. Bloomsbury Publishing USA, 2001.

2

THE ROLE OF TECH AMBASSADORS IN MODERN DIPLOMACY

Historical Context and Evolution

THE HISTORICAL EMERGENCE OF technology within the sphere of diplomacy has markedly transformed international relations in recent decades. From the telegraph and radio to the internet and social media, technological advancements have incessantly reshaped the diplomatic landscape. As states and global entities have recognized technology's profound influence on communication and information exchange, the role of tech ambassadors has adapted accordingly to address these multifaceted changes. Tech ambassadors are critical in representing their nations' interests within the digital milieu, tasked with responsibilities that include cultivating relationships with technology firms, advocating for policies that stimulate innovation and trade, and addressing pressing issues such as cybersecurity and data privacy on behalf of their governments ((Rana 2004). The delineation of these functions is essential in comprehending tech ambassadors' singular contributions to contemporary diplomacy. The convergence of technological progress and traditional diplomacy has heralded fresh prospects for cooperation and engagement. Amidst the proliferation of digital platforms and virtual interactions, tech ambassadors find themselves at the vanguard of integrating these instruments into diplomatic strategies. Numerous instances illustrate how tech diplomacy initiatives have borne fruit, from facilitating transnational collaborations on climate resilience to employing data analytics for humanitarian ventures during crises.(Mallik and For 2016)

Nevertheless, despite the potential advantages, tech ambassadors grapple with significant impediments and challenges in their diplomatic endeavors. Navigating intricate regulatory environments, bridging technological divides among nations, and fostering trust in an era plagued by cybersecurity anxieties constitute some hurdles that necessitate astute navigation (Rana 2004). Aspiring tech diplomats must hone a diverse skill set encompassing proficiency in emerging technologies, strategic negotiation skills, cultural awareness, and adaptability in rapidly changing contexts. Implementing recommended training programs designed to cultivate these competencies is imperative, thus equipping future tech ambassadors with the requisite expertise. (Sandre 2015)

Synergy and collaboration between tech ambassadors and traditional diplomatic officials are crucial for cohesive and effective diplomatic initiatives. Joint endeavors leveraging the strengths inherent in both domains can yield impactful policy outcomes that address the dynamic intersection of technology and international relations. The influence of tech ambassadors is increasingly pivotal in shaping international policy frameworks, as they furnish insights and perspectives informed by their profound understanding of the technological landscape. (Robertson and Janice Gross Stein 2011)

Looking forward, the evolution of tech diplomacy unveils intriguing possibilities for future developments and trajectories. As technological innovation continues unabated, tech ambassadors are positioned to play an integral role in navigating emerging challenges while harnessing the potential of transformative technologies. This section offers a comprehensive overview of the historical context and evolution of tech ambassadors, elucidating their indispensable contributions to modern diplomacy.(Venugopalan Ittekkot and Jasmeet Kaur Baweja 2023)

Defining the Role of Tech Ambassadors

In the rapidly evolving terrain of modern diplomacy, the designation of tech ambassadors has emerged as a vital element in shaping international relations. These ambassadors are entrusted with the mandate to bridge the chasm between the technological industry and diplomatic circles, harmonizing endeavors to navigate the intricate nexus of technology and global politics. At the core of a tech ambassador's role is leveraging technological advancements to foster cooperation, ameliorate conflicts, and tackle global predicaments (Burke 2012). This multifaceted role necessitates individuals equipped with an in-depth comprehension of both technological intricacies and the subtleties of international diplomacy. (Sandre 2015)

Among the primary responsibilities of tech ambassadors is the advocacy for their respective countries or organizations within the international tech arena. This responsibility entails articulating policy stances, championing national interests, and facilitating collaborations on technological ventures aligned with broader diplomatic aspirations. Furthermore, tech ambassadors function as principal conduits for dialogue, negotiation, and strategic partnerships within the global tech ecosystem, playing a pivotal role in shaping the trajectories of international tech policies (Burke 2012).

Moreover, the role of tech ambassadors transcends traditional diplomatic channels, embracing innovative methodologies for engagement and influence. They catalyze a digital innovation and entrepreneurship culture, propelling economic growth and enhancing global digital inclusion. By advocating for principles of transparency, ethical technology usage, and open communication, tech ambassadors fortify trust and mutual comprehension among diverse stakeholders, thereby solidifying the grounds for international collaboration ((Rana 2004).

Engaged at the cutting edge of technological domains such as artificial intelligence, cybersecurity, blockchain, and advanced manufacturing, tech ambassadors' expertise enables them to traverse complex regulatory landscapes, predict emerging risks, and harness the potential of disruptive technologies to advance shared global objectives—all while adhering to established international norms and standards (Rana 2004).

In essence, the role of tech ambassadors transcends mere representation; it encapsulates a visionary perspective anchored in technology's transformative capacity to engender positive changes on the world stage. As this discourse unfolds, we shall delve deeper into the particular strategies, competencies, and ethical considerations underpinning the effective execution of this pivotal role in contemporary diplomacy. (Venugopalan Ittekkot and Jasmeet Kaur Baweja 2023)

The Intersection of Technology and Diplomacy

The intricacies of modern diplomacy are now inextricably entwined with technological advancements, signaling a significant evolution in international relations. As the digital epoch unfolds, technological innovations redefine how nations interact and fundamentally alter the nature of conflicts, alliances, and negotiations. The convergence of technology and diplomacy encompasses myriad dimensions, each playing a crucial role in shaping the global diplomatic landscape.(Singh 2023)

A key aspect of this intersection is the impact of digital communication tools on diplomatic interactions. Platforms such as social media, video conferencing, and encrypted messaging have revolutionized how diplomats communicate with foreign counterparts. The immediacy of these exchanges facilitates swift responses to crises, enhances coordination during international engagements, and augments access to diverse viewpoints. However, this heightened reliance on digital communications also introduces challenges concerning cybersecurity, data privacy, and misinformation, necessitating careful navigation by tech ambassadors and diplomats alike (Sandre 2015).

Furthermore, the proliferation of emergent technologies like artificial intelligence, blockchain, and quantum computing ignites rigorous discourse regarding their ramifications on international diplomacy. These innovations offer the potential for streamlining diplomatic processes—such as expeditious visa applications, secure information exchanges, and strengthened cross-border collaborations—while concurrently provoking data security concerns, algorithmic biases, and potential disruptions to classical diplomatic norms. An astute comprehension of the strategic implications of such innovations is imperative for tech ambassadors as they navigate the intricate web of international relations.(Venugopalan Ittekkot and Jasmeet Kaur Baweja 2023)

Additionally, the rise of tech-enabled public diplomacy has transformed how nations project their soft power and engage with global audiences. Digital storytelling, virtual cultural exchanges, and interactive online initiatives have broadened the reach and efficacy of diplomatic outreach (Sandre 2015). This transformation necessitates that tech ambassadors adeptly utilize digital platforms and analytics to craft compelling narratives promoting their countries, fostering cultural awareness, and countering misinformation.(Robertson and Janice Gross Stein 2011)

Moreover, the amalgamation of technology and diplomacy extends to humanitarian assistance and crisis response territories. The application of technology significantly enhances the efficiency and effectiveness of diplomatic endeavors aimed at confronting global challenges, exemplified by the deployment of drones for delivering aid in inaccessible regions and the utilization of big data to predict and mitigate natural disasters. Nonetheless, tech ambassadors must ensure that technology-driven interventions adhere to ethical standards and respect the sovereignty of affected nations. (Singh 2023)

Overall, the intersection of technology and diplomacy presents unparalleled opportunities alongside intricate challenges. This paradigm necessitates the skillful navigation and strategic foresight of tech ambassadors as they engage in contemporary diplomatic arenas.

Case Studies: Successful Tech Diplomacy Initiatives

In the swiftly changing landscape of modern diplomacy, tech ambassadors have assumed pivotal roles in initiating and executing successful tech diplomacy initiatives. These case studies provide invaluable insights into how technology has emerged as a potent instrument for fostering international cooperation and addressing global challenges (Sandre 2015).

One prominent case study illustrates the collaboration between leading tech enterprises and various governments to counter disinformation and safeguard the integrity of democratic processes. Through innovative technological solutions, these partnerships have significantly bolstered digital resilience and mitigated the impact of malicious influence operations.

Equally compelling is the effective implementation of cross-border data-sharing agreements facilitated by tech ambassadors. By deftly maneuvering through intricate regulatory frameworks and addressing privacy concerns, these initiatives have enabled the seamless flow of data for research, cybersecurity, and public safety, thus promoting international collaboration and innovation.(Venugo palan Ittekkot and Jasmeet Kaur Baweja 2023)

Moreover, joint initiatives aimed at advancing sustainable development through the strategic deployment of technology stand as a testament to the impactful role of tech ambassadors. By harnessing digital solutions such as renewable energy technologies, smart infrastructure, and e-governance platforms, these initiatives have markedly contributed to attaining sustainable development goals across national boundaries. (Singh 2023)

Additionally, tech diplomacy initiatives have proven instrumental in facilitating humanitarian aid and crisis response efforts. Employing drones to deliver medical supplies in remote locales, utilizing social media platforms to raise awareness during natural disasters, and deploying advanced communication technologies to coordinate relief operations have showcased the invaluable impact of technology in addressing humanitarian crises.(Robertson and Janice Gross Stein 2011)

The success of these case studies exemplifies the transformative potential of tech diplomacy in overcoming global challenges and fostering mutual cooperation among nations. As tech ambassadors continue to navigate the complexities of international relations, these compelling narratives serve as guiding beacons for future initiatives, emphasizing the paramount role of technology in reshaping the diplomatic landscape.

Challenges Faced by Tech Ambassadors

Tech ambassadors face many challenges in their roles as modern diplomatic representatives tasked with navigating the complex intersection of technology and global affairs. One significant hurdle is the rapid pace of technological advancement, which often surpasses the ability of traditional diplomatic structures to comprehend and address emerging issues effectively (Bahl, 2021). This necessitates the continuous adaptation and upskilling of tech ambassadors to maintain relevance in a landscape characterized by constant innovation and disruption.(Venugopalan Ittekkot and Jasmeet Kaur Baweja 2023)

Moreover, technology's inherently borderless nature challenges traditional notions of territorial sovereignty and jurisdictional boundaries. Tech ambassadors must grapple with the complexities of cross-border data flows, digital trade, and cyber governance, all of which transcend conventional diplomatic frameworks and require a nuanced understanding of both technology and international relations.(Robertson and Janice Gross Stein 2011)

Another critical challenge lies in balancing the competing interests of diverse stakeholders, including tech corporations, civil society, governments, and multilateral organizations. Navigating these varied interests while upholding ethical standards and advancing national or supranational objectives demands astute negotiation skills and a deep comprehension of the intricate interplay between technology, politics, and economics.

Cybersecurity's challenge to tech ambassadors is critical since the increasing number of cyber threats and vulnerabilities highlights the need to promote protection and resilient digital environments. However, in accomplishing such targets beyond technical skills, one needs to possess the ability to encourage collaboration, foster confidence, and develop norms on responsible behavior of states in cyberspace.

Add to that the fact that ethical treatment of technological advancement raises more problems for technical concepts, ethical issues on privacy invasion, algorithm abuse, AI and biotech use, innovation in the context of economic development and growth, in general, employ a lot of applications. Moving into the future with ethical dilemmas while attempting to foster economic growth and innovation requires a level of appreciation of the technology's impact on society and adherence to sound ethics. (Singh 2023)

Additionally, tech ambassadors often confront the geopolitical dimensions of technology, including the risk of techno-nationalism, digital protectionism, and the weaponization of information and communication technologies. Striking a delicate balance between harnessing the benefits of technological interconnectedness and safeguarding national interests against potential threats demands adept strategic foresight and diplomatic acumen.

In conclusion, tech ambassadors' multifaceted challenges underscore the need for a dynamic and agile approach to modern diplomacy. Adapting to rapid technological shifts, navigating complex global dynamics, and fostering meaningful collaboration across sectors are imperative for tech ambassadors to fulfill their pivotal role in shaping the future of international relations.(Robertson and Janice Gross Stein 2011)

Skill Set Requirements and Training Programs

In modern diplomacy, the role of tech ambassadors demands a unique and diverse skill set that integrates technological expertise with traditional diplomatic acumen. Firstly, proficiency in various emerging technologies is essential, encompassing areas such as artificial intelligence, cybersecurity, blockchain, and digital communication platforms. A comprehensive understanding of these technologies enables tech ambassadors to represent their nation or organization effectively in discussions and negotiations related to tech policies and collaborations (Venugopalan Ittekkot and Jasmeet Kaur Baweja, 2023).

Strong communication skills are also imperative for articulating technical concepts to non-technical stakeholders, fostering international relationships, and promoting dialogue among diverse groups (Gora, 2021). Cultural intelligence and language proficiency are also crucial, as tech ambassadors often operate within global contexts and must navigate cross-cultural communication efficiently.(Singh 2023)

Moreover, thinking critically and strategically about technology's geopolitical implications is vital. This includes recognizing potential security risks, ethical concerns, and the broader socio-economic impacts of technological advancements. Beyond the technical domain, negotiation, mediation, and conflict resolution skills are indispensable, given the complex diplomatic landscape in which tech ambassadors operate. (National Research Council et al. 2015)

As tech diplomacy evolves, adaptability, resilience, and a commitment to lifelong learning are key qualities that can enable ambassadors to navigate unforeseen challenges and opportunities (Hassan, 2023). Given the specialized nature of this role, training programs tailored specifically for tech diplomats have emerged. These programs typically integrate elements of technology, international relations, law, and diplomacy (Bachir, 2021). They simulate real-world scenarios, enabling participants to develop practical skills for managing tech-related issues within a diplomatic framework.(Singh 2023)

Collaborative exercises, case studies, and role-playing simulations provide insights into navigating complex diplomatic negotiations in the context of evolving technologies. Furthermore, exposure to ethical dilemmas and decision-making frameworks enhances tech ambassadors' moral and ethical preparedness. Intensive language courses and cultural immersion experiences are often incorporated into these programs to foster an appreciation for diverse perspectives and ensure effective cross-cultural communication. Mentorship by seasoned diplomats and technologists offers valuable guidance and insight into the intricate dynamics of tech diplomacy.

Continuous professional development through workshops, seminars, and conferences is also emphasized, allowing tech ambassadors to stay abreast of the latest technological advancements and global policy shifts. By honing these skills and engaging in comprehensive training programs, tech ambassadors are better equipped to navigate the nuanced intersection of technology and diplomacy, thereby enhancing their effectiveness in representing their nations' interests amidst rapidly evolving global landscapes. (Mallik and For 2016)

Collaboration with Traditional Diplomatic Entities

In modern diplomacy, the collaboration between tech ambassadors and traditional diplomatic entities is paramount for addressing complex global challenges (Ahmad, 2020). While tech ambassadors bring a deep understanding of technological advancements and their implications, traditional diplomats possess extensive experience navigating geopolitical landscapes and building relationships with foreign governments.(Robertson and Janice Gross Stein 2011)

Collaboration between tech ambassadors and traditional diplomats entails exchanging knowledge and expertise to effectively address issues at the intersection of technology and international relations. (National Research Council et al. 2015) Traditional diplomats can provide valuable insights into different regions' political and cultural nuances, offering essential context to tech ambassadors navigating sensitive technological diplomacy initiatives. Conversely, tech ambassadors bring innovative solutions and a forward-looking approach, augmenting traditional diplomatic efforts with cutting-edge technological perspectives.

Furthermore, this collaboration fosters a more comprehensive and nuanced understanding of global challenges, allowing for the development of holistic strategies that integrate both traditional and tech-based diplomatic approaches. Joint efforts can create symbiotic partnerships where each party leverages its unique strengths to achieve common diplomatic objectives. Formal mechanisms for information sharing and joint decision-making processes must be established to facilitate this collaboration. This may involve creating joint task forces, organizing regular workshops, or integrating tech-focused modules into traditional diplomatic training programs.(Singh 2023)

Open communication channels and mutual respect are crucial in nurturing a productive and harmonious working relationship between tech ambassadors and traditional diplomats. Embracing diversity in expertise and perspectives becomes the cornerstone for successful collaboration. By acknowledging the complementary nature of their roles, both tech ambassadors and traditional diplomats can leverage their respective strengths to wield a more impactful diplomatic influence on the global stage. Through collaboration, these entities can ensure that the formulated policies and decisions encompass a balanced amalgamation of technological innovation and diplomatic finesse, ultimately advancing global peace and prosperity.(National Research Council et al. 2015)

Impact on International Policies

As the role of tech ambassadors continues to gain prominence in modern diplomacy, their impact on international policies cannot be understated. Integrating technology into diplomatic efforts presents a paradigm shift in how nations interact and shape global policies. These tech ambassadors serve as catalysts for innovation and collaboration, influencing the formulation and implementation of international policies across various domains.

One significant impact lies in the realm of trade and economic relations. Through leveraging technology, tech ambassadors can facilitate cross-border transactions, streamline customs procedures, and promote e-commerce, thereby contributing to the expansion and diversification of global trade (Walani, 2022). Additionally, they play a pivotal role in addressing regulatory discrepancies and fostering harmonization in international trade laws, ensuring fair and equitable participation of nations in the global marketplace. (Singh 2023)

Furthermore, in security and defense policies, tech ambassadors contribute to developing cybersecurity measures, laying the groundwork for international cooperation in combating cyber threats and ensuring the integrity of critical infrastructure. Their expertise in emerging technologies also enables them to advise on the intersection of national security and technological advancements, guiding the formulation of policies to safeguard sovereign interests while embracing innovation.(Robertson and Janice Gross Stein 2011)

Moreover, tech ambassadors' influence extends to environmental and sustainable development policies. By harnessing technological solutions, they can advocate for eco-friendly practices, monitor climate change impacts, and drive international collaboration towards achieving sustainable development goals. This includes promoting renewable energy initiatives, mitigating environmental risks through advanced monitoring systems, and facilitating knowledge transfer to bolster environmentally friendly policies worldwide.(Robertson and Janice Gross Stein 2011)

In the realm of human rights and humanitarian efforts, tech ambassadors leverage technology to amplify voices, uphold digital freedoms, and address the socio-ethical implications of technology adoption (Zakat, 2023). They champion policies prioritizing privacy protection, combating online censorship, and advocating for the ethical use of AI and biotechnology, thus shaping international conventions safeguarding human rights in the digital age.

Overall, tech ambassadors' impact on international policies transcends traditional diplomatic boundaries, ushering in an era of tech-driven diplomacy that resonates across economic, security, environmental, and ethical domains, thereby shaping a more interconnected and progressive global landscape.(Mallik and For 2016)

Future Trends in Tech Diplomacy

The advancement of technology continues to revolutionize diplomacy, presenting a wave of future trends that will shape the landscape of international relations. As we look ahead, several key trends emerge, providing insight into the evolving role of technology in diplomatic endeavors. (National Research Council et al. 2015)

Firstly, integrating virtual reality (VR) and augmented reality (AR) into diplomatic practices is poised to redefine how nations engage with one another. Virtual meetings and simulations can offer immersive experiences, transcending geographical barriers to facilitate more nuanced and impactful diplomatic interactions. This trend enhances communication and fosters greater mutual understanding among nations.

Secondly, the rise of blockchain technology can potentially transform how diplomatic agreements and transactions are conducted. Its immutable and transparent nature could instill a new level of trust and efficiency in international negotiations, trade, and aid distribution. Furthermore, the emergence of quantum communication technologies presents opportunities for highly secure and resilient channels for diplomatic communications (National Research Council et al. 2015). Quantum encryption techniques could mitigate cybersecurity risks and safeguard sensitive diplomatic exchanges.

Another significant trend on the horizon is the increasing influence of tech-savvy citizen diplomats. With social media and digital platforms empowering individuals to participate in global conversations, the traditional hierarchical structure of diplomacy is being reshaped. As a result, governments will need to adapt and engage with grassroots digital diplomacy efforts to effectively address public sentiments and opinions.

Additionally, the ethical implications of emerging technologies and their impact on human rights are poised to become focal points in diplomatic discourse. Issues such as data privacy, AI ethics, and biotechnology regulations will necessitate collaborative international efforts to establish ethical frameworks and guidelines.

Finally, the growing prominence of space diplomacy and the commercialization of space exploration introduce a new frontier for technological diplomacy. As nations and private entities venture into space, governance, and cooperation in this domain will require innovative diplomatic approaches.

In summary, the future of tech diplomacy holds promise for transformative advancements in communication, negotiation, and collaboration on the global stage. Understanding and leveraging these upcoming trends will be integral for shaping a more interconnected and technologically astute diplomatic landscape.

References:

- Burke, Lee H. "Ambassador at Large: Diplomat Extraordinary." Springer Science & Business Media, 2012.

- Ittekkot, Venugopalan, and Jasmeet Kaur Baweja. "Science, Technology and Innovation Diplomacy in Developing Countries." Springer Nature, 2023.

- Mallik, Amitav, and Institute For. "Role of Technology in International Affairs." New Delhi: Pentagon Press, 2016.

- National Research Council, Policy and Security, and Committee on. "Diplomacy for the 21st Century." National Academies Press, 2015.

- Rana, Kishan S. "The 21st Century Ambassador." Diplo Foundation, 2004.

- ———. "21st-Century Diplomacy." Bloomsbury Publishing USA, 2011.

- Robertson, Colin, and Janice Gross Stein. "Diplomacy in the Digital Age: Essays in Honour of Ambassador Allan Gotlieb." Toronto: Signal, 2011.

- Sandre, Andreas. "Digital Diplomacy: Conversations on Innovation in Foreign Policy." Lanham: Rowman and Littlefield, 2015.

- Singh, Ishwar. "The Code of Connection." Pencil, 2023.

3

TECH GIANTS AS GEOPOLITICAL ACTORS

Corporate Geopolitics

In an era marked by rapid technological evolution, sizable technology corporations have ventured into the domain of international politics, exercising sway that was once reserved for nation-states. The trajectory from the Cold War to the present digital epoch has seen these entities increasingly mold geopolitical dynamics. The amalgamation of technological innovations with global affairs has not only redefined traditional power hierarchies but also compelled these corporations to navigate intricate diplomatic and regulatory landscapes deftly. The ascendancy of Silicon Valley titans and other tech conglomerates as formidable actors in global geopolitics attests to their economic influence and inventive prowess. Their impact transcends mere commercial pursuits, permeating fundamental facets of national security, trade relations, intellectual property rights, and, indeed, human liberties (Gersbach 2020). This metamorphosis has ignited a rigorous examination of the roles and duties of tech companies within the realm of international relations. As technology continues to catalyze profound societal transformations, it is paramount to scrutinize the repercussions of corporate involvement in geopolitics to understand better the challenges and opportunities these emerging power brokers present on the global stage. (Witt 2022)

Historical Context of Technology Companies in Global Affairs

The interwoven relationship between technology firms and global affairs can be traced back to the inception of the digital age, punctuated by critical milestones that have shaped the landscape of corporate geopolitics. One seminal moment transpired in the 1980s when the surge of personal computers and the advent of the Internet unlocked transformative opportunities for businesses, states, and societies. This era laid the groundwork for the emergence of tech giants as influential players on the international scene (Fritsch 2011). As the Internet evolved from its academic and research confines into a robust commercial platform, the strategies of these technology companies began to pivot towards global outreach and market ascendancy. The dot-com boom of the late 1990s further intensified this trajectory, propelling the rise of corporations that secured their status as household names. Concurrently, the convergence of telecommunications and information technology heralded mobile connectivity, fundamentally altering the global communication dynamics.

At the dawn of the new millennium, the world witnessed the birth of businesses that redefined entire sectors and transcended geographic boundaries, amassing unparalleled economic clout. Silicon Valley, in particular, became synonymous with unparalleled innovation, attracting talent and investment from diverse locales. A pivotal inflection point emerged with the meteoric rise of social media platforms, which have dramatically influenced public discourse and geopolitical events. (Witt 2022) These platforms shatter traditional barriers, facilitating a previously inconceivable scale of communication and connectivity. The nexus of technological advancement and globalization propels technology firms into multifaceted roles within global affairs, spanning economic, political, and societal dimensions. (Watkins 1997)Understanding the historical evolution of these entities is crucial for grasping their contemporary influence and navigating the complexities of corporate geopolitics in the digital era. (Zhukov 2021)

Economic Influence and Market Dominance

The economic sway and market preeminence of tech giants in the global arena have fundamentally restructured established power paradigms and reshaped the dynamics of international trade and commerce. These corporations have achieved unprecedented levels of market control, often straddling diverse sectors, including technology, finance, entertainment, and communications. Their capacity to accumulate vast financial resources and exert significant influence on consumer behavior has positioned them as pivotal actors in the orchestration of the global economy. Their impact on both advanced and emerging markets is profound, as they can disrupt established industries and create new economic frameworks. (Fritsch 2011)

The sheer magnitude and reach of these tech titans empower them to leverage economies of scale, driving competition and innovation while simultaneously raising alarms about monopolistic practices and anti-competitive behaviors. Their sprawling global supply chains and intricate networks of partnerships have solidified their status as key players in the interconnected web of international trade. This intertwining of economic power with geopolitical ramifications demands a discerning understanding of the delicate balance between corporate interests and national sovereignty.

As these technology behemoths navigate regulatory landscapes and legal systems across various nations, myriad complexities emerge, prompting inquiries about equitable competition, consumer protection, and ethical business practices. The strategic allocation of financial resources, technological expertise, and proprietary data amplifies their capacity to influence policy-making and shape legislative agendas, thereby blurring the lines between economic power and political authority. In this milieu, the economic imprint of tech giants transcends conventional market dynamics, intersecting with societal welfare, labor practices, and resource distribution, thereby stimulating multifaceted discussions on wealth distribution, income inequality, and corporate social responsibility. Thus, a comprehensive analysis of their economic influence and market dominance is imperative to understand their cross-sectoral impacts, structural inequities, and the implications for global economic governance in the digital epoch. (Zhukov 2021)

Tech Giants' Role in International Diplomacy

Within the swiftly shifting landscape of international diplomacy, technology giants have emerged as formidable players, wielding significant influence that reverberates across global relations. The integration of technology into quotidian life has conferred upon these corporations a pivotal role in shaping not only economic policies but also diplomatic initiatives on a worldwide scale. Tech giants engage in international diplomacy through multifaceted conduits, leveraging their extensive resources, technological expertise, and global footprint to cultivate relationships with governments, international organizations, and various stakeholders.

Their engagement stretches beyond traditional business dealings; they actively participate in dialogues addressing trade agreements, data privacy regulations, and digital infrastructure development. These corporations frequently assume roles as thought leaders and advisors, providing valuable insights into the ramifications of emerging technologies for geopolitical dynamics. Furthermore, the services and platforms offered by these tech titans function as conduits for cultural exchange, information dissemination, and public discourse across borders. This positions them as potent influencers of global narratives and societal currents, further entwining their operations with diplomatic objectives.(Watkins 1997)

By initiating projects such as digital inclusivity programs and fostering cross-border partnerships, tech companies amplify their diplomatic presence, nurturing connections and shaping worldwide perceptions. However, their prominent involvement in international diplomacy engenders complex questions regarding the balance of power and accountability. As private entities, their motivations and actions may not always align with the strategic interests of nation-states, potentially breeding tensions or conflicts. (Wheeler 1969) Issues surrounding data sovereignty, intellectual property, and regulatory compliance present intricate challenges that intersect with traditional diplomatic considerations.(Zhukov 2021)

Moreover, the expanding sway of tech firms in global affairs necessitates new collaborative and governance frameworks. Conventional diplomatic actors must negotiate the nuances of engaging with these entities while ensuring adherence to established norms and principles of international relations. Concurrently, tech firms face mounting pressure to exhibit responsible and ethical conduct in their international dealings, especially amid rising surveillance, censorship, and disinformation concerns. As technology continues redefining diplomacy's underpinnings, the roles and responsibilities of tech giants within global governance will undoubtedly be subjects of extensive discourse and negotiation. Although their contributions can catalyze positive advances in international partnership and progress, the intricate interplay between technology and diplomacy necessitates continuous scrutiny and strategic dialogue to optimize benefits while mitigating risks. (Gersbach 2020)

Impact on National Security: Friend or Foe?

As technology giants amplify their global presence and influence, their ramifications on national security have spawned intense scrutiny and debate. On one hand, these firms have been instrumental in advancing the digital infrastructure and communications networks essential for modern national defense and intelligence operations. Their avant-garde technologies and expertise have empowered governments to bolster their cybersecurity measures, counter burgeoning cyber threats, and execute surveillance and reconnaissance endeavors. (Wheeler 1969) Furthermore, tech firms have partnered with governmental agencies to create and implement cutting-edge encryption methods and secure communication channels, thereby enhancing national security infrastructures. (Gersbach 2020)

Conversely, these corporations' proliferation of sophisticated surveillance tools and data analytics platforms raises serious concerns about potential privacy violations and unauthorized information access, posing substantial challenges to national security. The growing incorporation of foreign-manufactured hardware and software into critical infrastructures and military systems presents vulnerabilities that adversarial entities could exploit, thereby further jeopardizing national security (Zhukov 2021). Moreover, these tech corporations' global nature makes them susceptible to geopolitical strife, which may lead to disruptions in essential services and technologies, potentially compromising the resilience of national security frameworks. Amidst these complexities, achieving equilibrium between harnessing the technological acumen of these companies for national security interests while safeguarding against potential risks remains a significant challenge for policymakers and security professionals globally. (Fritsch 2011)

Collaborations with Governments and Global Institutions

As one of the most powerful bodies in the world, technology companies often partner with governments and institutions to effectively participate in policy-making and decision-making. These diverse partnerships cover national security, economic, digital opening, and even global governance. The growing number of joint projects of technology giants and governments creates as many questions as it attempts to settle the issues of sociopolitical relations. (Wheeler 1969)

A critical facet of these collaborations is the involvement of technology companies in public-private partnerships to address urgent global challenges (Zhukov 2021). Through joint undertakings, these entities forge alliances with governmental agencies and non-governmental organizations to confront issues like cybersecurity, climate change, and public health crises. By leveraging their expertise and resources, tech firms contribute significantly to formulating and implementing innovative solutions benefiting societies. However, the profundity of these collaborations sparks questions about the asymmetric power dynamics potentially emerging from the coalescence of technology and governance. (Watkins 1997)

Moreover, tech giants frequently engage in dialogues with global bodies such as the United Nations, the World Bank, and the International Monetary Fund. Such interactions allow them to express their perspectives on critical issues and propose industry-specific recommendations for policy frameworks. While such engagements can yield valuable insights and technical expertise, they also raise concerns about the accountability and transparency of these influential entities in shaping international agendas. Striking a balance between harnessing technological potential and preserving democratic principles remains an imperative in this c ontext.(Fritsch 2011)

Within national security, collaborations between tech firms and governments extend to surveillance, intelligence gathering, and military applications (Zhukov 2021). The deployment of advanced defense and law enforcement technologies underscores the necessity of comprehensive ethical guidelines and oversight mechanisms. Maintaining a balanced approach to security imperatives vis-à-vis individual privacy rights is an ongoing challenge, requiring informed deliberation and regulatory frameworks that align with global human rights standards. This involves recognizing the innovative capabilities of tech firms and holding them accountable for adhering to universal ethical principles. (Gersbach 2020)

While these collaborations offer opportunities for knowledge exchange and collective problem-solving, it remains crucial to critically assess the implications of such entanglements for democratic governance, social inclusivity, and individual freedoms. The intricate interplay between technology, governance, and society necessitates a nuanced approach that acknowledges the complexities of contemporary geopolitical landscapes while striving to integrate ethical considerations into these collaborative efforts. (Heaven 2019)

Ethical Considerations and Public Accountability

Tech giants face significant ethical challenges in the realm of techplomacy. Data privacy and user security are major concerns, with companies acquiring vast amounts of personal data. This raises questions about privacy infringement and potential misuse of sensitive information. Tech firms must balance their commercial goals with ethical responsibilities to protect user privacy.(Heaven 2019)

Content moderation and censorship present complex ethical dilemmas for tech corporations operating across diverse cultures and political systems. Regulating content without infringing on freedom of expression is a contentious issue requiring careful ethical navigation. (Wheeler 1969)

The impact of technology on employment and labor practices is another ethical concern. Job displacement, worker treatment, and societal implications of automation and AI are scrutinized, especially in regions where tech giants have large operational footprints. (Gersbach 2020)

Environmental sustainability and corporate social responsibility are also key ethical considerations. Tech infrastructure's energy consumption and electronic waste generation necessitate a shift towards sustainable practices and responsible development. As influential global entities, tech companies are expected to uphold high standards of environmental stewardship and contribute to addressing climate change.

Public accountability is closely tied to ethical considerations. Transparency in decision-making, stakeholder engagement, and participation in public discourse are essential for maintaining accountability. This extends to fair competition, anti-trust regulations, and corporate governance, significantly affecting market dynamics and economic equity.

Embracing public accountability requires building trust and credibility among stakeholders, including governments, consumers, and advocacy groups. Tech giants must align their corporate practices with broader societal values and interests. (Zhukov 2021)

Regulatory Challenges and Compliance

Tech giants face complex regulatory challenges in their global operations. They must navigate varying regulations across jurisdictions, covering data privacy, antitrust laws, intellectual property rights, and trade policies.

Disparate regulatory requirements across countries pose a significant challenge. Some nations prioritize strict data protection, while others favor unrestricted data flow for innovation and economic growth. This creates a dilemma for tech companies trying to maintain ethical standards while complying with diverse regulatory frameworks.(Heaven 2019)

Antitrust compliance is another major challenge. Tech giants' dominant positions have led to scrutiny from regulatory authorities aiming to prevent anti-competitive practices. Compliance requires proactive engagement with regulators and a commitment to transparency and accountability. (Wheeler 1969)

Intellectual property rights and trade policies further complicate the regulatory landscape. Disputes over patents, copyrights, and trade barriers can become diplomatic issues, requiring careful navigation to avoid legal entanglements and diplomatic conflicts. (Watkins 1997)

Emerging global regulatory trends, such as the extraterritorial application of data protection laws and localization mandates, add complexity to compliance efforts. Tech giants must adapt to different regulatory environments while maintaining ethical and corporate responsibilities. (Fritsch 2011)

Effective regulatory compliance in global tech operations requires proactive engagement with policymakers, diplomatic skills, and a comprehensive approach to legal conformity. Tech companies must navigate the interplay between geopolitical factors and regulatory frameworks to foster positive relationships with governments and regulators worldwide. Prioritizing ethical conduct and transparent compliance practices is crucial for maintaining public trust and long-term success in corporate geopolitics.(Zhukov 2021)

Case Studies: Notable Incidents and Initiatives

To elucidate the multifarious role of tech giants as geopolitical entities, it is essential to explore specific case studies that exemplify their influence on global affairs. One particularly significant incident pertains to a data privacy scandal involving a major social media platform. Unauthorized access to and exploitation of user data engendered substantial ethical and legal concerns across multiple jurisdictions. This incident illuminated the extensive repercussions of technology firms on individual privacy and prompted heightened scrutiny from regulatory agencies and governments globally.(Heaven 2019)

Moreover, the initiative undertaken by a prominent e-commerce corporation to invest in sustainable energy resources and mitigate its carbon footprint serves as a salient example of corporate accountability in addressing environmental challenges. This strategic move positioned the company as a frontrunner in sustainability within the tech sector and illustrated how technology giants exert considerable influence beyond conventional business domains.

Furthermore, technology companies' engagement in cross-border data governance issues underscores the complexities of navigating regulatory environments and international relations. By examining these case studies, we derive valuable insights into the intricate interplay between tech giants and global dynamics, emphasizing the necessity for nuanced approaches to understanding and engaging with these influential actors. (Zhukov 2021)

Future Projections: The Evolving Role of Tech Giants

The inexorable march of technological titans into the geopolitical arena heralds a paradigm-shifting transformation of global power dynamics. These digital behemoths, wielding unprecedented influence through their mastery of emerging technologies, stand poised to fundamentally reshape the traditional frameworks of international relations and societal governance (Heaven 2019).

In this rapidly evolving landscape, tech giants' tentacles extend beyond their traditional digital domains, penetrating crucial sectors like biotechnology, quantum computing, and sustainable energy. While promising revolutionary solutions to humanity's most pressing challenges, this expansion raises thorny questions about the concentration of power and the blurring lines between corporate interests and national sovereignty (Watkins 1997).

The regulatory labyrinth facing these technological leviathans grows increasingly byzantine, demanding sophisticated navigation through competing jurisdictional claims and conflicting international standards. This regulatory complexity catalyzes novel forms of corporate diplomacy, where tech giants must delicately balance innovation with compliance and market dominance with social responsibility (Zhukov 2021).

The ethical dimensions of this technological hegemony demand urgent scrutiny. As these entities increasingly shape global narratives and influence societal norms, their decision-making processes must incorporate robust ethical frameworks that transcend mere profit motives. The emergence of novel collaborative ecosystems between tech giants, governmental bodies, and civil society organizations presents a promising avenue for harmonizing corporate objectives with the public good.

The trajectory of tech giants' geopolitical influence appears bound for further amplification, yet with mounting calls for accountability and transparency. This evolution necessitates a delicate equilibrium between technological innovation and societal welfare, corporate autonomy and public oversight, and global reach, as well as local responsibility. The future landscape will likely witness unprecedented power-sharing arrangements, where traditional state authority interweaves with corporate technological capability in previously unimagined ways (Watkins 1997).

As these digital titans continue their ascent in the global power hierarchy, their actions will increasingly reverberate through international diplomacy, economic policy, and social development corridors. The ultimate challenge lies in harnessing their transformative potential while ensuring their alignment with broader human interests and values.

References

- Fritsch, Stefan. "Technology and Global Affairs." International Studies Perspectives 12, no. 1 (2011): 27–45. https://doi.org/10.1111/J.1528-3585.2010.00417.X.

- Gersbach, Hans. "Democratizing Tech Giants! A Roadmap." Economics of Governance 21, no. 4 (2020): 351–61. https://doi.org/10.1007/S10101-020-00244-5.

- Heaven, Douglas. "Taking on the Tech Giants." New Scientist 242, no. 3228 (2019): 18–19. https://doi.org/10.1016/S0262-4079(19)30778-X.

- Watkins, James D. "Science and Technology Foreign Affairs." Science 227, no. 5326 (1997): 650–51. https://dialnet.unirioja.es/servlet/articulo?codigo=427495.

- Wheeler, Gordon E. "Civic Affairs — How Deeply Should Companies Be Involved?" Management Decision 3, no. 1 (1969): 34–36. https://doi.org/10.1108/EB000881.

- Witt, Anna C. "Taming Tech Giants." The Antitrust Bulletin 67, no. 2 (2022): 187–89. https://doi.org/10.1177/0003603x221084153.

- Zhukov, D. "Tech Giants versus Nation States: Prospects for Digital Multipolarity." Journal of International Analytics 5, no. 2 (2021): 29–44. https://doi.org/10.12737/2587-6295-2021-5-2-29-44.

4

NAVIGATING ISSUES OF STATE SOVEREIGNTY IN THE DIGITAL AGE

Digital Sovereignty

Digital sovereignty emerges as a kaleidoscopic nexus where state power collides with the ethereal realm of cyberspace, birthing unprecedented paradoxes of control and autonomy. This crystallization of authority in the digital domain transcends mere technological oversight, manifesting as a complex tapestry of data governance, information architectures, and cyber-territorial claims that fundamentally reshape traditional power dynamics.

In this complex landscape, nations grapple with an existential tension: the imperative to assert control over their digital destinies while navigating cyberspace's inherently borderless nature. This dialectic spawns fascinating contradictions as governments simultaneously embrace and resist the centrifugal forces of digital globalization, crafting intricate frameworks that attempt to reconcile sovereign authority with the fluid, interconnected reality of modern technological ecosystems.

The digital revolution has catalyzed a profound metamorphosis in state functionality, unleashing a cascade of transformative ripples across the governance spectrum. As data flows transcend geographic boundaries with quantum-like unpredictability, tech titans emerge as quasi-sovereign entities, wielding influence that challenges traditional power structures. This creates a fascinating dance of authority between state actors and digital behemoths, each vying for influence in the virtual commons while negotiating the boundaries of their respective domains.

Within this volatile matrix, digital sovereignty manifests as a multidimensional construct, encompassing everything from cryptographic autonomy to algorithmic governance. It demands a delicate balancing act between national security imperatives and global digital integration, forcing states to architect sophisticated regulatory frameworks that can adapt to the quantum leaps of technological evolution. This dynamic interplay between digital rights and state power creates a fascinating crucible where the relentless tide of technological innovation continuously reshapes traditional governance models.

Historical Context: Sovereignty and the Evolution of State Control

The concept of sovereignty, a cornerstone of modern statecraft, traces its labyrinthine roots through the tumultuous emergence of nation-states in the 16th and 17th centuries. In 1648, the watershed Treaty of Westphalia - born from the ashes of the devastating Thirty Years' War - crystallized fundamental principles that would shape global politics for centuries to come. At its core, sovereignty embodies a deceptively simple yet profound idea: absolute authority within defined borders. But nothing is ever that straightforward.

The digital revolution has utterly transformed this centuries-old paradigm. Gone are the days when physical boundaries could neatly contain state power. In their place, we find ourselves navigating an intricate web of virtual connections that pay no heed to traditional borders. How can a nation truly control its "territory" when data flows like water through the cracks of any digital wall?

The intersection of technological advancement and global interconnectedness has spawned unprecedented challenges. States grapple with invisible threads of influence that weave across continents in milliseconds. Money zips through digital channels, information cascades across borders, and power dynamics shift like sand beneath our feet. These aren't just abstract concerns - they're reshaping the very foundation of governance.

The historical trajectory from territorial sovereignty to today's digital realm tells a fascinating story. Short, sharp disruptions punctuate long periods of gradual evolution. Traditional governance principles strain and bend under the weight of technological change, forcing adaptation at a breakneck pace that would have been unimaginable to the architects of the Westphalian system. Yet here we are, watching as states scramble to assert control in cyberspace while still clinging to centuries-old concepts of authority.

This digital metamorphosis demands our attention. As virtual landscapes reshape global politics with stunning velocity, understanding sovereignty's historical context becomes not just an academic exercise but a practical necessity. The past illuminates our path forward, even as we venture into uncharted territory where jurisdiction blurs, power relationships evolve, and policymakers face challenges that would baffle their predecessors.

Digital Sovereignty: Definitions and Interpretations

In our hyper-connected world, digital sovereignty has emerged as a captivating battleground where nations wrestle with control over their virtual domains. Picture this: a country striving to maintain its digital independence while data streams flow ceaselessly across invisible borders. At its essence, digital sovereignty encompasses a nation's capability to govern its digital realm autonomously - from data management to infrastructure control, from cybersecurity to information flows (Hellmeier et al., 2023).

The interpretation of digital sovereignty varies dramatically across the global stage, like a prism refracting light in countless directions. Some nations clutch it tightly as a shield against cultural erosion, a bulwark against the relentless tide of globalization that threatens to wash away their distinctive identities (Burri et al., 2022). Others, perhaps more pragmatic, view it through the lens of security—a vital tool in their arsenal against lurking cyber threats.

Here's where it gets interesting: the rise of tech giants has thrown a wrench into the traditional machinery of state power. These digital behemoths, concentrated in just a handful of countries, wield influence that would make historical empires blush. This unprecedented consolidation of digital authority has set off alarm bells in capitals worldwide, spurring calls for more robust regulatory frameworks (Hellmeier et al., 2023).

The plot thickens when we consider international relations. Digital sovereignty doesn't exist in a vacuum - it's inextricably tangled with global governance, creating a complex dance between national autonomy and international interdependence. This delicate ballet raises thorny questions: Where do we draw the lines of state power in cyberspace? How do we balance data flows with privacy rights? What about trade and human rights? (Burri et al., 2022)

Make no mistake - digital sovereignty is no static concept. Like mercury, it shifts and adapts as technology rapidly reshapes our world. Regional dialogues crackle with energy while international forums buzz with debate. The goal? Forging shared frameworks that can accommodate diverse perspectives and interests in this rapidly evolving digital landscape. Yet consensus remains elusive as nations navigate this brave new world with varying degrees of caution and enthusiasm.

Case Studies: National Approaches to Digital Sovereignty

The digital domain has become a fascinating theater where nations wage subtle wars of control and influence. To truly grasp the essence of digital sovereignty, we must dive deep into the labyrinth of strategies different countries employ to maintain their grip on virtual territories (Mainwaring et al., 2020). Gone are the simple days when borders were marked by stones and fences - now, they're defined by firewalls and data policies.

Think about it: as our world becomes increasingly interconnected, nations are forced to perform a delicate balancing act. Traditional notions of sovereignty, once carved in stone, now melt like ice in the digital heat. This transformation hasn't been gentle; it's pushed governments to their creative limits, compelling them to forge novel solutions for unprecedented challenges (Mainwaring et al., 2020).

The global landscape presents us with a remarkable tapestry of approaches. China, Russia, and the European Union are particularly intriguing case studies, each painting their digital sovereignty with distinctly different brushstrokes. Take China, for instance - its approach is nothing short of comprehensive. Like a master weaver, the nation has crafted an intricate web of regulatory frameworks, weaving together strict internet content oversight, sophisticated information filtering systems, and a robust national cybersecurity architecture guarding its digital frontiers (McCarthy et al., 2019).

These varying strategies tell us something profound about the nature of digital sovereignty itself. Some nations build virtual walls, while others create complex regulatory mazes. Short, decisive policies punctuate lengthy, nuanced frameworks. It's a dynamic dance of control and adaptation, where each country moves to its own rhythm while responding to the global beat of technological change.

The result? A patchwork of digital governance as diverse as the nations themselves, each approach reflecting unique cultural values, political priorities, and security concerns. This isn't just policy - it's a revolution in how we think about national boundaries and state power in our increasingly virtual world.

Challenges Posed by Global Tech Companies

In the landscape of digital sovereignty, transnational tech behemoths have emerged as formidable sovereignty-shapers, wielding unprecedented influence that transcends traditional geopolitical boundaries. These digital leviathans operate with stunning agility across jurisdictional matrices, their distributed architectures defying conventional regulatory frameworks and challenging the very essence of state authority (Maelen V et al., 2020).

The asymmetric power dynamics between nation-states and these corporate titans manifest in multifaceted ways - from algorithmic governance to data hegemony. These entities, armed with computational prowess surpassing many nation-states, orchestrate vast digital ecosystems that reshape the conventional paradigms of territorial control and governmental authority (Lundström et al., 1997).

At the epicenter of this sovereignty paradox lies the commodification of data - the new oil of the digital age. These corporations harvest, aggregate, and weaponize unprecedented volumes of granular personal information, creating sophisticated behavioral architectures that transcend traditional surveillance capabilities. This data supremacy engenders profound questions about privacy sovereignty and the emerging contours of digital citizenship.

The economic gravitational pull of these technological juggernauts warps market dynamics with devastating efficiency. Their platform economies create regulatory blind spots that traditional state mechanisms struggle to illuminate. Their ability to arbitrage regulatory frameworks across jurisdictions undermines conventional oversight paradigms, forcing a fundamental recalibration of sovereign authority.

The transformation of information ecosystems through digital platforms has catalyzed a seismic shift in narrative control and information sovereignty. The viral proliferation of disinformation, computational propaganda, and extremist ideologies presents an existential challenge to societal cohesion and democratic stability, compelling states to navigate the treacherous waters of content governance (Maelen V et al., 2020).

As nations grapple with these multidimensional challenges, the imperative for regulatory evolution becomes increasingly acute. Policymakers must orchestrate a delicate ballet between fostering innovation and preserving sovereign interests while navigating the complex interplay of competition law, consumer protection, intellectual property rights, and democratic values.

The crystallization of transnational coalitions and harmonized regulatory frameworks is a crucial counterbalance to tech giants' disruptive influence on state sovereignty. As technological evolution accelerates, the synthesis of governmental authority, industry expertise, and civil society engagement becomes paramount in architecting a digital commons reconciling national sovereignty with technological advancement.

Regulatory Responses and Legislative Measures

In today's digital age, big global tech companies present significant challenges that require strong regulatory actions and laws to support national sovereignty and address new issues. Governments worldwide face the tough task of balancing tech firms' creative freedom with the need to protect national interests and oversee their operations within country borders.

Countries have taken different paths in regulating digital platforms and tech companies, looking to find a fair balance between fostering innovation and ensuring oversight. Some governments have established strict data protection laws and antitrust rules to reduce tech companies' monopolistic practices, promote fair competition, and protect consumer privacy (March C et al.). Other nations have focused on creating clear policies that outline what these companies must do while ensuring a balance between technological progress and compliance with national laws (March C et al.).

Regulations to improve digital sovereignty cover various actions, from creating data localization laws to restrictions on international data flow and taxes specifically for digital services. These efforts aim to strengthen control over data ownership, enhance cybersecurity measures, and address the economic inequalities caused by the power of large multinational tech firms (Cohen et al., 2006).

Furthermore, cooperation among governments and regulatory bodies worldwide is crucial to address broad issues and promote a unified approach to digital governance. Agreements between countries are essential for setting rules for cross-border data sharing, cybersecurity efforts, and resolving conflicts that arise from different regulatory systems.

Policymakers must carefully balance encouraging innovation and protecting national interests through their regulatory actions. As technology changes, adjusting and improving laws to maintain state sovereignty while navigating the complicated relationship between technology and governance will be vital. This requires ongoing discussions, proactive policy development, and flexible frameworks that can tackle the challenges of the digital era.

International Cooperation and Conflict Over Digital Jurisdiction

In an era of unprecedented digital interconnectivity, traditional notions of jurisdiction undergo radical metamorphosis. The ubiquitous nature of cyber interactions has catalyzed fierce contestation regarding jurisdictional boundaries' scope and limitations, particularly concerning transnational data flows and cyber incidents (Mishago et al., 2012). As digital architectures evolve with dizzying velocity, governments grapple with the labyrinthine challenge of delineating and enforcing jurisdictional parameters within an inherently borderless digital ecosystem (Kettemann et al., 2020), spawning both formidable obstacles and unprecedented opportunities for multilateral collaboration and dispute resolution.

International Cooperation

The complexities of digital jurisdiction have precipitated widespread recognition among nation-states regarding the imperative for synchronized regulatory frameworks addressing critical spheres like data protection, cybersecurity enforcement, and cross-border information access (Hare et al., 2019). States endeavor to orchestrate regulatory harmonization and fortify information-sharing mechanisms through intricate bilateral and multilateral diplomatic arrangements, thereby enhancing their collective capacity to navigate transnational challenges (Félix et al., 2017). Such initiatives cultivate inter-state trust and mutual comprehension and catalyze coordinated responses to cross-jurisdictional incidents.

Conflict Over Digital Jurisdiction

Despite robust collaborative initiatives, divergent national interests and competing jurisdictional paradigms frequently ignite intense interstate tensions, particularly regarding data privacy frameworks, surveillance protocols, and content governance mechanisms (Hulvey et al., 2023). The absence of universally embraced standards exacerbates these challenges, spawning contentious debates over extraterritorial application of domestic legislation and state authority in cyberspace (McCarthy et al., 2019). Left unaddressed, these jurisdictional friction points threaten to undermine global stability and impede the development of cohesive international digital governance frameworks.

Future Prospects

Resolving digital jurisdictional complexities demands innovative diplomatic paradigms and steadfast adherence to fundamental principles of international law (Félix et al., 2017). Striking an equilibrium between national sovereign prerogatives and universal standards proves crucial for maintaining harmonious interstate relations in the digital domain (Fergusson et al., 2010). Simultaneously, ensuring transparent and inclusive digital governance policy formulation processes becomes paramount for fostering trust and reconciling divergent jurisdictional perspectives. Leveraging multilateral forums and diplomatic channels to facilitate dialogue and negotiation remains essential for mitigating tensions and promoting collaborative oversight of cross-border digital operations.

Balancing National Security and Individual Privacy

In the era of rapid digital evolution, the intricate dance between national security and personal privacy has emerged as a contentious battleground for governments, organizations, and individuals across the globe. Swift technological advancements have unveiled myriad methods for monitoring society while simultaneously spawning various cyber threats that challenge conventional notions of sovereignty and privacy (Mainwaring et al., 2020). As nations strive to shield their citizens from external dangers, they are entangled in the convoluted web of digital rights and personal liberties.

Central to this debate is the profound tension that exists between the imperatives of robust national security measures and the necessity of safeguarding fundamental individual rights. Governments frequently advocate for enhanced surveillance and extensive data harvesting as indispensable tools in the fight against terrorism, cyber threats, and myriad other global perils (McCarthy et al., 2019). Conversely, privacy advocates vehemently underscore the critical importance of protecting individual rights, championing the notion of freedom from relentless intrusion. Thus, navigating the delicate balance between these opposing interests is vital for upholding democratic tenets while ensuring the populace's security.

As this debate unfolds, it acquires greater urgency, particularly when addressing the complexities of international collaboration and intelligence sharing. Nations reconcile disparate legal frameworks and cultural perspectives on privacy, data protection, and surveillance practices. The burgeoning tide of cross-border data transactions amplifies the necessity for coherent international standards governing personal information collection, retention, and usage.

Moreover, technological advancements—ranging from sophisticated encryption and anonymization tools to the burgeoning realm of blockchain—pose additional challenges for law enforcement and national security operatives. While such innovations herald improved privacy safeguards, they simultaneously erect formidable barriers for authorities attempting to thwart illicit activities and preserve national security (Mainwaring et al., 2020).

This discourse necessitates a comprehensive approach, wherein resolving the conflicts between national security and individual privacy demands the establishment of clear legal frameworks. These frameworks should uphold privacy rights, delineate the bounds of surveillance activities, and institute robust oversight mechanisms. Equally imperative is the collaborative synergy among governments, technologists, and civil society, aiming to forge standards that mitigate security risks without encroaching upon individual freedoms.

The ramifications of this precarious equilibrium extend beyond mere policy and legal discourse; they resonate through public sentiment, foster global trust in institutions, and shape the trajectory of future technological innovations. Acknowledging the intricate interrelation between national security and individual privacy is, therefore, essential for cultivating substantive dialogues, enhancing understanding, and promoting responsible governance in this increasingly digital landscape.

The Role of International Organizations in Digital Governance

The dynamics of international organizations within the digital governance sphere manifest through an intricate web of paradoxical influences and kaleidoscopic power structures. These entities, operating at the nexus of technological innovation and geopolitical machinations, orchestrate an elaborate dance of sovereignty negotiation and normative architecture (Beck U et al., 2014). The digital realm's ethereal nature defies traditional territorial bounds, compelling these organizations to craft novel paradigms that transcend conventional governance frameworks.

In this byzantine landscape, international bodies catalyze the crystallization of digital norms through multifaceted engagement mechanisms. The United Nations Group of Governmental Experts exemplifies this complexity, weaving together disparate threads of cybersecurity doctrine, data sovereignty principles, and international legal frameworks into a tapestry of evolving digital governance (Irion et al.). This intricate process oscillates between periods of rapid evolution and prolonged deliberation, reflecting the underlying tensions between technological acceleration and institutional inertia.

The capacity-building imperative manifests through labyrinthine networks of knowledge transfer, where asymmetric power relations intersect with technological disparities. These organizations navigate treacherous waters between empowerment and dependency, orchestrating complex interventions, and bridging and highlighting digital divides. Their multistakeholder approach generates a cacophony of voices - governmental, civil, corporate, and technical - creating a dynamic tension that both enriches and complicates policy formulation.

As technological frontiers expand exponentially, these organizations perpetually recalibrate their roles amidst shifting paradigms. The digital governance landscape morphs unpredictably, demanding adaptive responses to emergent challenges while maintaining coherent frameworks for international cooperation. This perpetual flux engenders both opportunities for innovation and risks of institutional obsolescence.

The future trajectory of international organizations in digital governance remains enigmatic, shaped by competing forces of fragmentation and consolidation. Their influence oscillates between periods of transformative impact and relative impotence, reflecting the volatile nature of digital sovereignty in an interconnected world. This dynamic equilibrium between order and chaos continues to define their essential yet precarious position in global digital governance.

Strategic Implications for Future Digital Policies

In digital governance, emerging regulations cast long shadows across the global technoscape, where sovereignty interweaves with innovation in increasingly Byzantine patterns (Amoretti et al., 2015). The kaleidoscopic nature of technological evolution demands regulatory frameworks that possess chameleonic adaptability, morphing seamlessly with each quantum leap in innovation while maintaining robust safeguards against the hydra-headed threats of cybersecurity breaches and truth-distorting misinformation cascades.

The intricate choreography of inclusive policy-making pirouettes precariously between disparate stakeholders - from labyrinthine governmental bureaucracies to silicon-powered tech titans, from grassroots civil society movements to ivory tower intellectuals. This complex tapestry of voices must harmonize across borders, weaving international standards that bridge the yawning chasms between jurisdictional frameworks while preserving local autonomy.

In the enforcement arena, accountability mechanisms must evolve beyond mere legal constructs, embracing multidimensional oversight that encompasses ethical considerations, human rights preservation, and democratic values (Lopez A, 2008). These mechanisms must function like a neural network, adapting and responding to violations precisely while maintaining the delicate balance of digital ecosystem health.

The horizon bristles with technological revolution - quantum computing's reality-bending potential, AI's ever-expanding consciousness, and biotechnology's genome-altering capabilities demand prescient policy architecture. These emerging paradigms necessitate regulatory frameworks that can anticipate seismic shifts while remaining sufficiently flexible to absorb unprecedented innovations without fracturing.

Digital literacy is crucial, demanding sophisticated educational initiatives that transcend basic skills to foster critical thinking and cyber-resilience. This empowerment must penetrate all societal strata, creating an informed citizenry capable of navigating the treacherous waters of digital manipulation and exploitation (Amoretti et al., 2015).

The strategic implications cascade through multiple technological, sociopolitical, and economic dimensions, creating a complex matrix of interdependencies that demand nuanced policy responses. Success in this digital labyrinth requires unprecedented collaboration among global stakeholders, ensuring that regulatory frameworks are catalysts for innovation while maintaining robust protective barriers against emerging threats.

References:

- Amoretti, Francesco, and Mauro Santaniello. "Universidad Católica de Colombia. Facultad de Derecho." 2015. https://core.ac.uk/download/213561036.pdf.

- Antonio Lopez. "The MacArthur Foundation Digital Media and Learning Initiative." 2008. https://core.ac.uk/download/71339822.pdf.

- Beck, U., M. Bevir, L.-V. Bril, C. Coker, K. Deutsch, B. Dupré, J. Ellul, et al. "'Informa UK Limited." 2014.

- Burri, Mira, Markus Christen, Bernice Elger, Christian Hauser, Marcello Ienca, Michele Loi, Christian Schneble, David E. Shaw, and Eleonora Vigano. 2022. https://www.zora.uzh.ch/id/eprint/225228/1/SSRN_id4081192.pdf.

- Cohen, Julie E. "Scholarship @ GEORGETOWN LAW." 2006. https://core.ac.uk/download/70374569.pdf.

- Cullell March, Cristina. 2024. https://core.ac.uk/download/pdf/6505069.pdf.

- Félix, Georges, Cristian Timmermann, and Pablo Tittonell. 2017. https://core.ac.uk/download/185244892.pdf.

- Fergusson, Ian F. "DigitalCommons@ILR." 2010. https://core.ac.uk/download/5131181.pdf.

- Hare, Paul Webster. "' Springer Science and Business Media LLC.'" 2019. https://open.bu.edu/bitstream/2144/

39129/4/CorrodingConsensusBuilding_AM.pdf.

- Hellmeier, Malte, and Franziska von Scherenberg. "AIS Electronic Library (AISeL)." 2023. https://core.ac.uk/download/567667291.pdf.

- Hulvey, Rachel, and Beth Simmons. "Penn Carey Law: Legal Scholarship Repository." 2023. https://core.ac.uk/download/572705594.pdf.

- Irion, Kristina. 2024. https://core.ac.uk/download/pdf/6618334.pdf.

- Kettemann, Matthias C. "'Oxford Brookes University'." 2020. https://core.ac.uk/download/343334506.pdf.

- Lundström, Niklas L.P., and Jonatan Vasilis. "Duke University School of Law." 1997. https://core.ac.uk/download/62564491.pdf.

- Mainwaring, Sarah. "' Cambridge University Press (CUP)'." 2020. https://core.ac.uk/download/323058085.pdf.

- McCarthy, Amy H., Mark Visger, and David A. Wallace. "DigitalCommons@UM Carey Law." 2019. https://core.ac.uk/download/212819600.pdf.

- Mishago, Tilahun. "GGU Law Digital Commons." 2012. https://core.ac.uk/download/233104379.pdf.

- Vander Maelen, Carl. "'Informa UK Limited'." 2020. https://core.ac.uk/download/287939745.pdf.

5

Impact of Social Media on International Relations

The Global Impact of Social Media: An Overview

IN MODERN DIPLOMACY, SOCIAL media's metamorphic influence has irrevocably altered the architecture of international relations, birthing an unprecedented paradigm where digital resonance amplifies geopolitical reverberations. This technological zeitgeist, characterized by its kaleidoscopic reach and velocity, has transcended conventional diplomatic parameters, forging a complex tapestry of instantaneous, borderless discourse that challenges traditional power hierarchies and information dissemination models.

The digital arena's transformative capacity manifests through its ability to catalyze seismic sociopolitical shifts, exemplified by watershed moments like the Arab Spring's cascading revolutionary wave and the global proliferation of the Black Lives Matter movement. These platforms have evolved into sophisticated instruments of statecraft, where nations orchestrate elaborate soft power strategies while navigating the treacherous waters of digital sovereignty and cybersecurity imperatives.

This digital diplomatic revolution presents a paradoxical duality. While it democratizes global discourse and accelerates cross-cultural pollination, it simultaneously fragments the information landscape, creating echo chambers that can amplify disinformation and polarization. The resultant ecosystem demands a nuanced understanding of how digital platforms reshape international relations, security paradigms, and global governance structures, compelling stakeholders to adapt to an environment where virtual influence often supersedes traditional diplomatic leverage. As this digital metamorphosis evolves, the intricate interplay between social media's connective tissue and geopolitical dynamics becomes increasingly central to understanding modern international relations.

The Evolution of Social Media Platforms

Since it started, social media has changed a lot, moving from simple online tools for talking to strong platforms that shape discussions worldwide and impact international relations. Early sites like Six Degrees and Friendster set the stage for the complex digital world we have today. However, platforms like MySpace, Facebook, and Twitter really changed how people connect and communicate globally (Boyle et al., 2016). These sites allowed personal interactions and became important for sharing news, influencing public opinion, and driving social and political movements.

As social media grew, new platforms emerged, each adding unique features. Visual platforms like Instagram and Snapchat took advantage of the trend of sharing images, while LinkedIn became the top site for professional networking and industry talk. The rise of video platforms, especially YouTube and later TikTok, expanded social media by allowing user-generated content to shape cultural trends. Furthermore, messaging apps like WhatsApp and Messenger changed private communication, blurring the lines between personal and work-related discussions.

Over the years, these platforms added new features like live streaming, augmented reality filters, and content curation based on algorithms, enhancing user engagement and their overall impact. Advances in mobile technology and better internet access have also been key in shaping social media, enabling users to stay connected at all times and anywhere. The widespread use of these platforms has not only affected how people behave and interact but has also become essential in international relations and diplomacy. This evolving nature of social media requires governments, organizations, and individuals to adjust, raising important issues about privacy, security, and the ethical use of digital power. Understanding how social media has changed is vital for seeing its current effects on international relations and managing the complex landscape of digital diplomacy and global communication.

Key Players and Their Influence on Public Opinion

Social media has emerged as a formidable force worldwide, fundamentally transforming the ways in which information circulates and how public opinions take shape. At the epicenter of this evolution are key individuals, groups, and platforms that wield tremendous influence over the sentiments of millions, steering international conversations and reshaping global narratives. The social media landscape, vast and multifaceted, thrives on the contributions of a diverse array of participants, each fulfilling a distinct role in shaping public discourse across borders.

Prominent among these contributors are influential figures—from political leaders and cultural icons to intellectual thought leaders—who leverage social media to communicate directly with global audiences in unimaginable ways. These individuals can galvanize large communities and energize public discourse, empowering them to shift narratives, advocate for critical causes, and influence transnational debates (D'Urso et al., 2018). Often seen as unofficial ambassadors for their respective countries or personal ideologies, they employ soft power tactics to shape international relations, drive policy discussions, and foster social change. Their presence on social media underlines the transformation of diplomacy, creating a new dynamic where leaders speak to their compatriots and a global audience.

Complementing these individual influencers are the media organizations and news agencies that have harnessed social media's expansive potential to elevate their reach and refine their narratives. The rise of citizen journalism and the proliferation of diverse channels for content dissemination have disrupted traditional models of journalism, amplifying a range of voices and perspectives (Campaign CC, 2014). While this democratization of information empowers individuals and communities, it also underscores a sobering reality: the rapid, unfiltered spread of misinformation. False narratives, which often snowball faster than facts, pose significant risks to global stability, underscoring the pressing need for ethical journalism and robust fact-checking mechanisms in the digital age.

Adding to the complexity of this ecosystem are the social media platforms themselves—powerhouses like Facebook, Twitter, and Instagram—that do far more than serve as communication hubs. These platforms capitalize on advanced algorithms to curate user experiences, thereby exerting immense control over the content people see and engage with. By shaping information flows, prioritizing certain narratives, and tailoring feeds to users' preferences, these platforms wield a quiet yet profound influence on shaping beliefs, guiding opinions, and framing the collective consciousness.

Beyond individuals and corporations, advocacy groups, NGOs, and grassroots movements have carved out a powerful presence in this digital arena. These organizations skillfully navigate social media to build support, drive awareness, and initiate policy changes at an unprecedented scale. Whether championing human rights, combating climate change, or promoting social equity, these groups have become adept at mobilizing global audiences and amplifying their voices through striking campaigns and digital engagement strategies. By curating emotionally resonant messaging and leveraging visual storytelling, they engage audiences in ways that traditional channels often cannot.

As one examines this intricate web of influential actors—spanning individuals, news outlets, social platforms, and advocacy organizations—it becomes apparent that their collective sway transcends borders, altering the fabric of international relations and diplomatic exchange. Social media has melded once-isolated spheres of influence into an interconnected ecosystem, where crafting and reshaping public opinion have become central to global engagement. Recognizing the dynamic interplay between these actors is essential for understanding the modern global discourse and developing strategies to effectively engage with a world increasingly entwined in the threads of digital communication.

Social Media as a Diplomatic Instrument

In this digitally supercharged era, social media has orchestrated an unprecedented metamorphosis of traditional diplomacy, birthing a kaleidoscopic landscape where nations and their representatives dance across virtual platforms with dizzying velocity (Hare et al., 2019). The once-staid corridors of diplomatic discourse have exploded into a labyrinthine network of tweets, posts, and shares, where ambassadors and foreign ministries pirouette through the delicate art of international relations with newfound immediacy and reach.

This digital renaissance has birthed a paradoxical symphony where formal diplomatic protocols collide with the raw authenticity of social engagement. Like master puppeteers, nations now choreograph their international personas through carefully curated digital narratives, wielding influence through a sophisticated arsenal of cultural storytelling and strategic messaging (Stahn et al., 2007). The diplomatic stage has expanded exponentially, transforming into a multilayered spectacle where every post becomes a potential catalyst for cross-cultural enlightenment or international tension.

Yet beneath this shimmering surface lurks a darker undercurrent. The same platforms that enable lightning-fast communication also serve as conduits for waves of misinformation, threatening to erode the bedrock of diplomatic credibility. In this chaotic ecosystem, diplomats must simultaneously serve as truth-tellers and digital warriors, defending against the viral spread of falsehoods while maintaining their delicate balance on the high wire of international relations.

The relentless pulse of social media has created an always-on diplomatic environment where traditional boundaries between public and private discourse have dissolved into a fluid continuum. Each digital interaction becomes a high-stakes performance, where a single misplaced character could ignite a diplomatic firestorm. This new reality demands an evolved form of statecraft—one that combines the wisdom of traditional diplomacy with the agility of digital engagement.

Despite these vertiginous challenges, digital diplomacy's transformative potential remains undeniable. It offers an unprecedented platform for fostering global dialogue and understanding, even as it demands constant vigilance and adaptation. As nations navigate this brave new world, success will hinge on their ability to harness the electric possibilities of social media while skillfully managing its inherent volatility—a delicate dance between opportunity and chaos in the ever-evolving theater of international relations.

Case Studies: Triumphs and Tribulations in Digital Diplomacy

The metamorphosis of diplomatic relations in our hyper-connected era has catapulted social media into an unprecedented position of influence, fundamentally revolutionizing the architecture of international discourse. This digital renaissance has birthed extraordinary diplomatic breakthroughs and catastrophic communication failures, weaving an intricate tapestry of consequences globally (Elbe et al., 2021).

Diplomatic Triumphs in the Digital Sphere

The Obama administration's masterful orchestration of social media engagement stands as a watershed moment in digital diplomacy. Their innovative deployment of platforms like Twitter and Facebook shattered traditional diplomatic constraints, forging direct pathways to global citizenry and catalyzing a paradigm shift in international relations (Webb et al., 2009). This groundbreaking approach didn't merely transmit messages; it fundamentally reconstructed the architecture of diplomatic engagement, cultivating unprecedented levels of transparency and accessibility.

The EEAS's Digital Diplomacy Division exemplifies another remarkable triumph, demonstrating extraordinary finesse in leveraging social media's connective tissue to amplify European Union policies. Their sophisticated digital strategy transcended conventional diplomatic boundaries, fostering vibrant cross-cultural dialogues and establishing new paradigms for multilateral engagement (Burchell et al., 2015).

Digital Diplomatic Disasters

Yet, the digital diplomatic landscape is treacherously complex. The Arab Spring illuminated the volatile nature of social media diplomacy, where authoritarian attempts to manipulate and suppress digital discourse backfired spectacularly. Nations like Egypt and Syria discovered that digital suppression often ignites rather than extinguishes dissent, triggering cascading diplomatic crises (Hare et al., 2019).

The virulent spread of misinformation presents an equally formidable challenge, with false narratives propagating at lightning speed through digital networks. This phenomenon has repeatedly overwhelmed traditional diplomatic responses, creating labyrinthine challenges for governments struggling to maintain credibility in an increasingly skeptical digital ecosystem (Stahn et al., 2007).

The Digital Diplomatic Frontier

As we navigate this complex digital terrain, the imperative for nuanced, sophisticated approaches to social media diplomacy becomes increasingly apparent. Success demands not just technological adoption but strategic wisdom in wielding these powerful tools. The future of international relations hinges on our ability to harness social media's transformative potential while deftly managing its inherent risks, crafting a new diplomatic paradigm for our interconnected age.

The Role of Social Media in Political Movements and Revolutions

In an unprecedented metamorphosis of political activism, social media has catalyzed a seismic disruption in the architecture of dissent, revolutionizing the very DNA of how populations mobilize, vocalize, and crystallize transformative change. The digital commons—a labyrinthine ecosystem of interconnected platforms—has emerged as an incendiary crucible where grievances ignite, resistance coalesces, and ossified power structures face relentless challenges (Shaw et al., 2001). The Arab Spring's digital inferno and Occupy's viral insurgency testify to social media's capacity to midwife epochal political convulsions.

These virtual agoras have become crucibles of empowerment for society's marginalized voices and resistance movements, amplifying their narratives through a kaleidoscopic array of digital megaphones while forging transnational solidarity networks. Contemporary activists weaponize an arsenal of digital tools—from viral hashtag storms to raw, unfiltered live streams and memetic campaign blitzkriegs—to spotlight systemic injustices and human rights violations, catalyzing global consciousness and compelling action from power brokers and international bodies (Ishkanian et al., 2007).

Moreover, social media's hyper-accelerated information ecosystem has shattered traditional gatekeeping monopolies, democratizing narrative creation and public discourse. This unmediated pipeline to global audiences has exponentially compressed the cycle of political storytelling, enabling grassroots voices to bypass institutional filters, expose corruption's shadowy machinations, and lay bare the machinery of oppression with unprecedented velocity and reach.

Challenges Within the Digital Landscape

In digital activism, social media platforms have metamorphosed into double-edged swords, simultaneously illuminating and obscuring truth's precarious path. These digital amphitheaters, while amplifying voices of change, paradoxically serve as fertile breeding grounds for synthetic narratives and calculated deception (Martin C et al., 2013). State actors and shadowy non-state entities weaponize these platforms, orchestrating byzantine campaigns of falsehood that corrode authentic grassroots movements.

Governments, wielding sophisticated digital arsenals, deploy multifaceted strategies - from surgical censorship to pervasive surveillance architecture and cybernetic intimidation - systematically dismantling opposition voices and controlling information cascades (McGovern et al., 2014). As social media's DNA mutates, political movements undergo parallel evolutionary transformations, their trajectory increasingly shaped by algorithmic amplification, precision-targeted messaging, and the thorny labyrinth of data privacy concerns.

Information Warfare: The Digital Battlefield of Hearts and Minds

In our hyperconnected epoch, the viral proliferation of fabricated narratives poses existential challenges to global diplomatic equilibrium. Contemporary information warfare, particularly within social media's echo chambers, represents a calculated assault on the collective consciousness, deliberately seeding chaos and institutional skepticism (Singh et al., 2024). This digital arms race, prosecuted by both sovereign powers and autonomous actors, engineers perception, foments discord and recalibrates geopolitical dynamics (Bajwa et al., 2021).

Misinformation Versus Disinformation: A Taxonomy of Deception

While misinformation propagates through innocent vectors of human error, disinformation represents calculated psychological operations designed to manipulate and deceive (Ceri et al., 2019). Both phenomena possess reality-warping potential, distorting policy landscapes and fracturing societal cohesion across borders. State-sponsored architects of deception, alongside independent disruptors, orchestrate increasingly sophisticated campaigns. Understanding their methodologies - from botnet deployment to synthetic identity farms and weaponized narrative engineering - becomes crucial in crafting effective countermeasures (Arntzen et al., 2010).

The ripple effects of information warfare permeate cybersecurity paradigms and national defense frameworks. As nations scramble to fortify their information sovereignty, specialized units emerge to counter malicious exploitation of digital information systems. Accelerating technological evolution amplifies the urgency of addressing both ethical imperatives and regulatory frameworks in combating information warfare. The delicate balance between preserving free expression while mitigating digital deception's toxic impact presents a formidable challenge.

This analysis examines paradigmatic cases of misinformation and disinformation campaigns, dissecting their operational mechanics and geopolitical ramifications. It scrutinizes the evolving responsibilities of technology platforms in containing false narratives while exploring governmental and societal obligations in fostering digital literacy and analytical thinking. Ultimately, navigating information warfare's complexity demands unprecedented cooperation across local, national, and global spheres to safeguard information integrity and nurture democratic discourse.

The Ethical Implications of Algorithmic Bias

Algorithmic bias is a big worry in technology and international relations. As digital tools and platforms become more common in global communication, the risk of bias in algorithmic decision-making raises important ethical issues. While algorithms help analyze and manage large amounts of data, leading to greater efficiency and automation, they also bring various challenges and ethical problems.

A major issue is that algorithms can carry social biases. In areas like predictive policing, hiring, and access to loans, algorithmic bias has been proven to unfairly hurt marginalized groups, worsening existing social inequalities (Bourne et al., 2021). This prompts important questions about fairness, justice, accountability, and responsibility in the tech industry.

A complete approach is needed to tackle algorithmic bias, requiring teamwork among tech experts, lawmakers, ethicists, and affected communities. Openness in algorithmic decision-making, careful auditing, and regular assessments are crucial to lessen bias's ethical impacts (Cameron et al., 2023). Additionally, promoting diversity and inclusivity in algorithms' design and development is vital for reducing built-in biases and achieving fairer results.

Global cooperation is key in setting standards and rules for responsible algorithm design and use, as this helps create a worldwide environment that respects ethical principles. Since algorithmic bias impacts many countries, addressing these ethical challenges requires collective efforts from both the public and private sectors. It is also important to create a culture of responsible innovation, where ethical factors are integral to technological progress, to ensure that algorithmic bias is actively reduced. By looking at the ethical effects of algorithmic bias from a global viewpoint, stakeholders can work toward building frameworks that emphasize equity, transparency, and accountability in the realms of technology and international relations.

Policy Responses and Regulatory Approaches

The rise of social media has fundamentally transformed international relations, demanding a nuanced and balanced approach to policy and regulation. A robust framework for content moderation plays a pivotal role in addressing the proliferation of misinformation, hate speech, and propaganda while safeguarding the principles of free expression. As Collison et al. (2019) emphasize, this task requires dynamic and ongoing collaboration among governments, technology companies, and civil society organizations, creating a multi-layered response to the challenges digital platforms pose.

Algorithmic transparency and accountability are now indispensable cornerstones of a fair and equitable digital ecosystem. With algorithms shaping global public opinion and information flows, the call for oversight mechanisms grows louder. Regulatory frameworks must remain agile, capable of adapting to the fast pace of technological developments while steadfastly protecting fundamental human rights and upholding democratic values. KA B et al. (2017) underscore that the inherently transnational nature of digital challenges—ranging from data privacy issues to cross-border misinformation campaigns and cybersecurity threats—requires harmonized international cooperation and standardized policy approaches to mitigate risks effectively.

The pathway to success lies in fostering multi-stakeholder engagement. Policymaking must encompass the insights of academia, industry leaders, civil society, and advocacy organizations, ensuring that policies are evidence-based and inclusive of diverse perspectives. Such holistic participation can craft solutions that resonate with the needs of the global digital community. In tandem, enhancing digital literacy and critical thinking capabilities across societies remains essential, empowering users to differentiate between credible information and manipulative content.

Hence, building a sustainable and ethical digital future necessitates innovative regulatory strategies that prioritize collaboration, adaptability, and inclusiveness. These efforts are vital to promoting trust in the global digital sphere and harnessing social media as a powerful tool for advancing diplomacy, fostering international cooperation, and strengthening global relations (KA B et al., 2017).

Future Trends and the Evolving Landscape

The trajectory of international relations is deeply interwoven with the evolution of technology and the digital sphere. As we look ahead, several key trends are poised to shape the intersection of technology and diplomacy, fundamentally altering how global actors connect and collaborate.

One pivotal trend is the emergence of new social media platforms and innovative communication tools, reshaping global dialogue among individuals, organizations, and nations (Hare et al., 2019). These platforms offer unprecedented opportunities for fostering international exchange but also amplify the risk of misinformation, polarization, and discord. Balancing these dual aspects will be essential for maintaining constructive global engagement.

Equally transformative is the accelerating adoption of artificial intelligence and machine learning in diplomatic processes such as data analysis, decision-making, and negotiation (Hare et al., 2019). While these tools promise greater efficiency and precision, they also provoke challenging ethical and security dilemmas, demanding vigilant oversight and nuanced governance.

Another significant shift is the growing influence of technology companies and non-governmental organizations in global affairs (Hare et al., 2019). This decentralization departs from purely state-centric diplomacy, inviting a more inclusive yet intricate power structure. As these non-traditional actors gain prominence, diplomatic norms must evolve to accommodate their expanding role while safeguarding international stability and equity.

Cybersecurity also looms as a critical concern, essential for protecting sensitive diplomatic communications and deterring malicious cyberactivity. A robust digital defense infrastructure is indispensable for sustaining trust and cohesion in a world increasingly dependent on interconnected systems (Cornish et al., 2017).

Moreover, the rapid pace of technological innovation consistently outpaces regulatory frameworks, creating an urgent need for adaptable policies that can effectively govern transformative technologies without stifling innovation. To navigate this uncharted territory, policymakers must strike a delicate balance between proactive regulation and fostering cross-border cooperation.

Finally, the proliferation of digital information ecosystems necessitates a renewed emphasis on digital and media literacy. Cultivating critical thinking skills and digital resilience will empower individuals to navigate complex online environments while mitigating the societal risks of disinformation and manipulation.

The successful navigation of these trends hinges on multilateral collaboration among governments, technology firms, civil society, and international organizations. By working collectively, these stakeholders can harness technological advancements to strengthen diplomacy, deepen mutual understanding, and drive constructive global outcomes—ensuring a future where innovation aligns with shared human values.

References:

- Hare, Paul Webster, "' Springer Science and Business Media LLC'," 2019, https://open.bu.edu/bitstream/2144/39129/4/CorrodingConsensusBuilding_AM.pdf

- Boyle, Raymond, "'Informa UK Limited," 2016, https://core.ac.uk/download/46560387.pdf

- D\u27Urso, Scott C., "e-Publications@Marquette", 2018, https://core.ac.uk/download/213089166.pdf

- Clean Clothes Campaign, "DigitalCommons@ILR", 2014, https://core.ac.uk/download/33619160.pdf

- Webb, Alban, 2009, https://core.ac.uk/download/81971.pdf

- Burchell, Kenzie, Gillespie, Marie, Nieto McAvoy, Eva, O'Loughlin, Ben, 2015, https://core.ac.uk/download/146487392.pdf

- Shaw, Martin, "' Cambridge University Press (CUP)'," 2001, https://core.ac.uk/download/2712425.pdf

- Ishkanian, Armine, "SAGE Publications Ltd," 2007, https://core.ac.uk/download/219913.pdf

- Bajwa, Aman, "Simon Fraser University Library, Canada & Canadian Association for Security and Intelligence Studies," 2021, https://core.ac.uk/download/482730009.pdf

- Singh, Sukhjinder, "Monterey, CA; Naval Postgraduate School," 2024, https://core.ac.uk/download/618458559.pdf

- Collison, David, Contrafatto, Massimo, Ferguson, John, Power, David, Stevenson, Lorna, "'Emerald'," 2019, https://core.ac.uk/download/286356098.pdf

- Bamberger K.A., Blyth M., Callon M., Claessens S., Cliff D., Currie W.L., Daniel P. Gozman, DeWalt K.M., Eaton B., Fields K., Flick U., Fligstein N., FSA, Geertz C., Gibson J.J., Glaser F., Golden B.R., Greenwald B.C. , Heidegger M., Jonathan J. M. Seddon, Krawiec K.D., Kvale S., Majchrzak A., Miles M.B., Patton M., Pettigrew A.M., Power M., Punch K.F., Saldana J., Schinckus C., Silverman D., Soin K., Solomon J., Tiejun M., van Li T., Wendy L. Currie, Yin R., "'Springer Science and Business Media LLC'", 2017, https://core.ac.uk/download/132168488.pdf

- Cornish, Hilary, Fransman, Jude, Newman, Kate, "Christian Aid," 2017, https://core.ac.uk/download/143477120.pdf

- Stahn, Andreas,, van Hullen, Vera., 2007, https://core.ac.uk/download/5080588.pdf

- Bourne, Clea D., Edwards, Lee, "De Gruyter Mouton", 2021, https://core.ac.uk/download/372706712.pdf

- Cameron, Lindsey, Lamers, Laura, Leicht-Deobald, Ulrich, Lutz, Christoph, Meijerink, Jeroen, Möhlmann, Mareike, "AIS Electronic Library (AISeL)", 2023, https://core.ac.uk/download/554503538.pdf

- Clifton Martin, Laura Jagla, "Aspen Institute Communications and Society Program," 2013, https://core.ac.uk/download/71361701.pdf

- Alyce McGovern, Sanja Milivojevic, "Justice and Social Democracy," 2014, https://core.ac.uk/download/pdf/30673177.pdf

- Ceri, Stefano, Pierri, Francesco, 2019, http://arxiv.org/abs/1902.07539

- Arntzen, Jenny, Krug, Don, "School of Information Technology Murdoch University," 2010, https://core.ac.uk/download/pdf/16436381.pdf

- West, Lauren Claire, "LSU Digital Commons," 2018, https://core.ac.uk/download/217417283.pdf

- Elbe, Stefan, "'SAGE Publications'," 2021, https://core.ac.uk/download/416688432.pdf

6

CYBERSECURITY AND THE INTERSECTION OF TECH AND POLICY

An Examination of Cybersecurity in the Contemporary Digital Epoch

The digital architecture that underpins every facet of modern life is both a marvel and a vulnerability. As the gears of technological progress spin ever faster, the shadow of cybersecurity threats grows longer and more intricate, reshaping how individuals, organizations, and nations understand and address risk. From the crude computer viruses of the past to the high-stakes game of ransomware, espionage, and state-sponsored cyber assaults of today, the evolution of these adversarial tactics has been nothing short of astonishing, marked by dramatic surges in scope, sophistication, and consequence. What once seemed confined to isolated technical glitches now looms as a global existential challenge.

Adapting to this relentless onslaught demands a foundational shift, one built on time-tested and evolving cybersecurity principles. Multifactor authentication isn't just a precaution; it's an imperative. Encryption serves as both a shield and a cipher of trust in an interconnected world, while the importance of proactive training—humanizing the technical defenses against phishing and deception—cannot be overemphasized. Yet, beyond individual best practices, government intervention has become inexorable. National and international policies are the new bastions of defense, laying frameworks that strive to balance security imperatives with ethical considerations and privacy rights. Laws on cybersecurity must evolve as swiftly as the digital threats they aim to counter, demanding a foresight that so often proves elusive in governance.

Still, cyberspace is not the preserve of any single actor or domain. The symbiosis of public and private sector collaboration has emerged as a critical force multiplier in the fight against cybercrime. Public initiatives may offer oversight and regulation, but it is private innovation that drives many of the technological breakthroughs necessary to combat threats. Swift information-sharing, the pooling of resources to counter global vulnerabilities, and the cross-pollination of expertise have proven invaluable in reinforcing defenses. On the international stage, treaties and cooperative agreements have become both the glue and lubricant of global cyber defense. Unified responses to emerging threats and the dissemination of shared lessons form the backbone of resilience, though the persistence of cyberattacks underscores the work yet to be done. Highly publicized data breaches and infrastructure disruptions are visceral reminders of the thin margins protecting critical digital arteries.

Looking toward an uncharted future, the challenges grow murkier. The rise of IoT devices—ubiquitous, interconnected, and often inadequately secured—offers new attack vectors shaping the cyber threat landscape of tomorrow. Layer onto this the advancing capabilities of AI, which swing like a double-edged sword, offering tools for defense but equipping adversaries with unprecedented weapons of exploitation. Meanwhile, the sheer dependence on critical infrastructure technologies means the stakes of failure now verge on catastrophic. With power grids, healthcare systems, and transportation networks hanging in a precarious balance, the mandate for preemptive strategy becomes glaringly urgent.

To sustain trust in the digital age, global cybersecurity must be not only strengthened but perpetually reimagined. Investments in cutting-edge security technologies, the pursuit of agile international alliances, and regulatory systems adaptive enough to mirror the tempo of innovation are indispensable. Cybersecurity will not merely be a technical field—it will anchor global stability in an era where the distinction between the physical and digital worlds grows ever hazier. In this space of rapid evolution, the unrelenting pursuit of resilience is no longer optional; it is survival.

The Historical Metamorphosis of Cyber Threats

Since the inception of computer networking, the landscape of cyber threats has undergone a dramatic transformation, evolving from harmless experimentation to sophisticated, multifaceted dangers. The origins of cybersecurity challenges trace back to the 1970s, an era when hacking was primarily an exploratory pursuit. Early hackers were trailblazers of the digital frontier, driven more by curiosity and the adrenaline of bypassing rudimentary networks than by malicious intent.

However, as computing technology advanced, so did the complexity and intent of cyber threats. The 1980s ushered in the age of computer viruses and worms, disruptive programs that began as mischievous experiments but quickly escalated in destructive capability. These early forms of malware hinted at the havoc that digital vulnerabilities could wreak, creating a foundation for the threats to come.

The 1990s represented a turning point as the proliferation of personal computers and mainstream internet access opened Pandora's box of new online dangers. Phishing scams, identity theft, and the exploitation of software vulnerabilities became rampant during this era, marking the transition from inconvenience to serious personal and financial harm. As Mobilio et al. (2024) note, these developments highlighted a growing sophistication among bad actors and their techniques, aligning with society's increasing digital dependency.

By the 2000s, cybercrime had evolved into a lucrative industry. The emergence of organized cybercriminal networks targeting individuals, corporations, and governments signaled a shift in priorities—from mayhem and mischief to profit-driven manipulation. Ransomware attacks, large-scale data breaches, and complex fraud schemes characterized this decade, underscoring the financial stakes of cyber vulnerabilities. Concurrently, state-sponsored cyber operations emerged as a geopolitical weapon of choice. Espionage, sabotage, and the destabilization of critical systems demonstrated the power of digital tools in modern conflicts, erasing the boundaries between physical and virtual battlegrounds.

The dawn of the 21st century's interconnectedness—marked by the convergence of critical infrastructure, global networks, and digitized everyday activities—introduced a labyrinthine web of vulnerabilities. The intricate and interdependent nature of these systems has heightened the stakes of cyber threats, elevating them to global security concerns. Nation-states, private organizations, and individuals must now contend with an adversarial landscape characterized by its relentless evolution and adaptability.

The trajectory of cyber threats underscores the urgency of staying ahead of an ever-shifting menace. Each milestone in this timeline reflects a broader lesson: that the digital realm is both a battleground and a proving ground, where technological advancements prompt equally innovative and disruptive responses. Understanding this evolution, as Mobilio et al. (2024) suggest, is integral to forging resilient cybersecurity frameworks capable of meeting tomorrow's challenges.

Essential Cybersecurity Protocols and Best Practices

In our labyrinthine digital landscape, implementing sophisticated cybersecurity protocols has become nothing short of existential. The kaleidoscope of cyber threats demands an intricate tapestry of defense mechanisms, where conventional safeguards interweave with cutting-edge countermeasures. At the vanguard stands the enigmatic realm of access governance—a complex orchestration of authentication paradigms that transcends simple password protection. The deployment of biometric-enhanced MFA, zero-trust architectural frameworks, and AI-driven behavioral analytics creates an almost impenetrable fortress against unauthorized infiltration (Fantin et al., 2020).

The cryptographic battlefield presents another fascinating dimension, where quantum-resistant algorithms dance with traditional encryption protocols in an elaborate security ballet. Data, whether dormant in digital vaults or traversing the global information highways, demands unprecedented protection against increasingly sophisticated adversaries. Meanwhile, the cybersecurity nerve center pulses with real-time threat intelligence, where machine learning algorithms scrutinize network patterns with almost prescient accuracy, distinguishing benign anomalies from malicious incursions (Radanliev et al., 2024).

Vulnerability assessment metamorphoses into an art form where ethical hackers probe digital fortifications with the finesse of master locksmiths. These digital stress tests reveal the hidden fissures in organizational defenses while simultaneously strengthening the human firewall through immersive security awareness programs. The human element, often the Achilles' heel of cybersecurity, transforms into a formidable asset through gamified learning experiences and scenario-based training.

In software development, security becomes an algorithmic symphony. DevSecOps practices weave protective measures into the very fabric of code while automated scanning tools conduct relentless interrogations of each line, hunting for potential vulnerabilities with mechanical precision. When security incidents inevitably pierce these defenses, orchestrated incident response protocols spring into action like well-rehearsed battle plans.

Cross-sector collaboration evolves into a cybersecurity ecosystem, where threat intelligence flows like digital lifeblood between organizations. This collective defense strategy, bolstered by regulatory frameworks and industry standards, creates a resilient shield against the dark arts of cyber warfare.

This multidimensional approach to cybersecurity—where technical innovation meets human intuition—forms the cornerstone of digital resilience. Organizations wielding these sophisticated tools and strategies navigate the treacherous waters of cyberspace with newfound confidence, contributing to a more secure digital future for all.

The Role of Government in Cyber Defense

In a dynamically shifting digital landscape where advanced technologies entwine opportunities with vulnerabilities, governments stand as the ultimate bulwark against the pervasive threats of cyber malfeasance. The gravity of their role lies in the formulation and enforcement of sophisticated cybersecurity policies—intricate blueprints that establish definitive protocols for both public and private entities, shaping the scaffolding of national safety in cyberspace (Renaud et al., 2019). These frameworks evolve into action through operationalized **national cybersecurity plans**, wherein governments delineate systematic approaches to detect, assess, and mitigate cyber risks (Igonor et al., 2020). Such plans are not merely procedural; they anchor their efficacy in strategic allocation of resources—funneling investments into cutting-edge defense mechanisms and nimble response strategies meticulously designed to neutralize cyber incursions with precision.

Yet, governance in cyberspace is not an isolated pursuit. The architecture of national defense is fortified through collaboration with an expansive network of stakeholders—spanning law enforcement agencies, intelligence units, and custodians of critical infrastructure. This intimate synergy forms a cohesive defensive shield capable of withstanding the relentless innovation of cyber adversaries. At the heart of this ecosystem lies the exchange of actionable intelligence. Via robust entities like **Computer Emergency Response Teams (CERTs)** and **Information Sharing and Analysis Centers (ISACs)**, governments construct agile conduits for sharing real-time threat intelligence across sectors. This proactive circulation of insights fosters early detection and swift countermeasures, blunting the potency of malicious campaigns and reinforcing systemic resilience.

Parallel to these defensive contours, governments recognize the indispensability of an enlightened and vigilant citizenry. Public awareness campaigns emerge as essential instruments in cultivating cyber hygiene, equipping individuals and businesses alike with the knowledge to identify and thwart emergent threats (Renaud et al., 2019). These initiatives not only instill preventative measures but amplify the collective responsibility of securing national digital ecosystems, bridging the gap between policy conception and societal engagement.

When breaches inevitably occur—as they often do in this asymmetrical theater of conflict—governments pivot to dynamic response modes. Armed with specialized cyber teams and advanced forensic technologies, agencies dive into the intricate aftermath of attacks, unraveling the complexities of breaches to pinpoint perpetrators, attribute motivations, and facilitate recovery. The velocity and precision of these operations determine not only the mitigation of immediate damage but also set the tone for long-term deterrence, signaling the cost of cyber aggression to adversarial actors.

Beyond their national frontiers, governments operationalize the principles of cyber diplomacy. In an interconnected domain where no country stands exempt from the cascading impacts of digital conflict, multilateral cooperation becomes imperative. By participating in global dialogues, advancing bilateral agreements, and championing normative frameworks for responsible cyber conduct, governments shape the ethos of cybersecurity on an international plane (Igonor et al., 2020). These diplomatic ventures do more than formalize cooperation; they enshrine collective accountability, threading transparency and stability into the agitated fabric of global cyberspace.

Ultimately, the government's role in cyber defense is one of perpetual evolution—balancing prescriptive policies with adaptive strategies, consolidating domestic hard power while forging international goodwill. Their endeavors encompass the full spectrum of anticipation, collaboration, response, and reform, ensuring that as the digital age grows increasingly volatile, national interests and global security remain safeguarded against omnipresent threats.

Public-Private Partnerships in Enhancing Cybersecurity

The landscape of cybersecurity defies traditional boundaries, manifesting as an intricate tapestry of shared vulnerabilities and collective imperatives. Public-private partnerships (PPPs) have crystallized as transformative frameworks, orchestrating an unprecedented fusion of governmental gravitas and private-sector dynamism to combat the kaleidoscopic nature of cyber threats (Aiken K). These symbiotic alliances acknowledge that digital risks cascade through the interconnected nervous system of modern civilization, threatening not just state apparatus but the very foundations of critical infrastructure—from financial arteries to healthcare matrices.

The architectural genius of PPPs lies in their ability to synthesize seemingly paradoxical strengths: the nimble innovation engines of private enterprise with the comprehensive regulatory machinery of state powers. Corporate titans, particularly those pioneering technological frontiers, function as sentinel outposts in the digital wilderness, their specialized knowledge systems enabling rapid threat detection and revolutionary countermeasures. This expertise, when interwoven with government intelligence apparatus, creates a formidable defensive matrix capable of neutralizing sophisticated, transnational cyber onslaughts (Zhang et al., 2020). The resulting synergy amplifies collective threat awareness, fostering an adaptive ecosystem where adversarial methodologies are decoded and countered with unprecedented precision.

These partnerships catalyze a revolutionary cross-pollination of cybersecurity protocols, transcending industrial silos while optimizing resource allocation. The emergence of unified threat intelligence platforms and synchronized response mechanisms has birthed a new paradigm in crisis management architecture.

Governmental entities, wielding unique powers of incentivization—through fiscal stimuli and legislative frameworks—forge international bridges that amplify global cyber resilience. This intricate dance of public and private capabilities dismantles the fragmentary barriers that historically impeded coordinated responses to large-scale digital incursions.

The collaborative alchemy of PPPs generates sector-specific security solutions that leverage diverse expertise portfolios. Technology behemoths and telecommunications architects craft sophisticated defense mechanisms for critical infrastructure, while government agencies deploy geopolitical acumen and diplomatic leverage against state-sponsored cyber warfare. This convergence of capabilities engenders a robust ecosystem of mutual reinforcement, fortifying both domestic and international security frameworks through strategic symbiosis.

However, the efficacy of these partnerships pivots on cultivating an environment of unprecedented trust and operational transparency. The establishment of standardized protocols for intelligence exchange and incident response becomes paramount in harmonizing sectoral objectives. Immersive training scenarios and threat simulation exercises forge operational cohesion, ensuring seamless coordination during actual cyber crises. Moreover, nurturing an atmosphere of psychological safety—where vulnerability disclosure carries no stigma—catalyzes proactive threat reporting, enriching the partnership's empirical foundation for threat mitigation strategies.

As the horizon of cyber threats expands—embracing quantum computing possibilities and artificial intelligence vectors—PPPs emerge as indispensable bulwarks against digital chaos. These dynamic collaborations must evolve continuously, pioneering innovative defense mechanisms while navigating regulatory labyrinths and technological asymmetries. By orchestrating this complex dance of public and private capabilities, PPPs architect a resilient shield protecting not just individual entities but the entire digital ecosystem underpinning contemporary civilization.

Legislation and Policy Frameworks for Cyber Defense

Cybersecurity, today, has become a top worry for governments, businesses, and individuals. Strong laws and policies are vital parts of an effective cyber defense plan to manage the challenges posed by cyber threats. These laws aim to set legal boundaries, clarify roles, and provide guidance on how to deal with cyber risks at both national and global levels.

At the national level, countries are working hard to create and update laws and rules to boost their cyber defense abilities. These actions cover a range of topics, including data privacy, requirements for reporting incidents, powers of law enforcement, and responsibilities linked to cyber events (Bank I-AD, 2016). Moreover, policy guidelines define the duties of government bodies, private organizations, and citizens in protecting critical infrastructure and sensitive data from cyber attacks (Woodall J et al.).

Working together internationally is essential to address cyber issues that cross borders. The nature of cyberspace requires unified agreements and treaties to promote cooperation, allow for the sharing of information, and standardize responsible state behavior in the digital arena. Efforts like the Budapest Convention on Cybercrime and the Tallinn Manual have begun to set a foundation for shared legal standards and principles on how states should act online.

Additionally, creating cyber defense policies needs a collaborative approach that brings together legal, technological, and strategic aspects. Policymakers should consult cybersecurity professionals, legal experts, industry leaders, and community groups to ensure laws and policies keep up with technological changes and evolving risks. This teamwork helps develop flexible frameworks that can effectively deal with the changing landscape of cyber threats.

While laws and policies set the stage for cybersecurity, ongoing evaluation and adjustment are crucial to meet new challenges. The fast pace of technological change, the rise of connected devices, and the increasing skill of cybercriminals create ongoing difficulties for current laws. Therefore, regularly reviewing and amending cyber defense policies is necessary to keep them effective and relevant in a constantly shifting digital world.

Strong laws and policy frameworks are essential for a solid cyber defense strategy. By outlining legal responsibilities, encouraging international teamwork, and embracing a collaborative approach, these frameworks help build a secure and resilient digital environment for governments, businesses, and individuals.

International Collaboration and Treaties on Cybersecurity

In global cybersecurity, the imperative for transnational synergy emerges as a beacon through the digital tempest. As malevolent actors pirouette across virtual borders with quicksilver grace, the antiquated paradigm of isolated national defense crumbles like digital sand castles before the tide of evolving threats.

The cybersphere's borderless expanse demands an intricate tapestry of collaboration, where nation-states must perform a delicate ballet of sovereignty and shared responsibility. Information cascades through neural networks of trust, while joint initiatives crystallize into multifaceted defensive architectures that transcend geographical constraints.

Consider the prismatic nature of modern cyber-cooperation:

- Quantum-encrypted intelligence highways pulsing with real-time threat matrices

- Cross-pollinated training ecosystems that birth hybrid defense methodologies

- Collaborative R&D crucibles forging tomorrow's digital shields

- Treaty frameworks that dance between rigid structure and fluid adaptation

Yet beneath this cooperative facade lurks a hydra of challenges: legal systems clash like tectonic plates, sovereignty concerns cast long shadows over data-sharing horizons, and technological evolution outpaces diplomatic deliberation with relentless momentum. The Budapest Convention stands as both beacon and battlefield, where nations negotiate the razor's edge between collective security and autonomous control.

As we hurtle toward an increasingly interconnected future, the architecture of international cyber-cooperation must evolve beyond static treaties into living, breathing ecosystems of trust and capability. Success demands a symphony of public-private partnerships, multilateral engagement, and adaptive governance frameworks that can pivot as swiftly as the threats they confront.

In this digital crucible, unity becomes both shield and sword - our collective defense against the gathering storm of cyber threats that recognize no borders, respect no boundaries, and render obsolete the very concept of isolated security.

Case Studies: Significant Cyber Attacks and Their Impacts

In cybersecurity, seismic digital catastrophes have fundamentally reconfigured our understanding of organizational vulnerability and global interconnectedness. Contemporary threat landscapes have evolved into Byzantine matrices of unprecedented sophistication, unleashing cascading perturbations across the cyber sphere.

The 2017 Equifax breach epitomizes this new paradigm - malicious actors, exploiting arcane application vulnerabilities, exfiltrated the personal data pantheon of 147 million souls. This digital cataclysm catalyzed not merely financial hemorrhaging but a profound erosion of consumer faith and regulatory metamorphosis (Arcuri et al., 2018).

The NotPetya ransomware apocalypse of 2018 orchestrated a symphony of chaos, devastatingly targeting critical infrastructure nexuses and corporate behemoths. This digital plague illuminated the gossamer-thin membrane between cyber and kinetic warfare, inflicting multibillion-dollar wounds across the global economy (Gastineau et al.).

Stuxnet's 2010 emergence heralded a paradigmatic shift in cyber warfare's ontology. This digital chimera, surgically targeting Iranian nuclear facilities, demonstrated the awesome potential for code to manifest physical devastation. Similarly, WannaCry's 2017 digital tsunami submerged hundreds of thousands of systems worldwide, exposing the fragile interdependencies of our hyperconnected techno-ecosystem.

These digital catastrophes serve as prophetic harbingers, demanding urgent cultivation of robust cyber-defense architectures and unprecedented international synchronization. As threat vectors grow increasingly byzantine, these historical crucibles illuminate the imperative for adaptive resilience and collective vigilance in our perpetually evolving digital battlespace.

Future Trends and Challenges in Cybersecurity

The accelerated evolution of technology, accompanied by its application in multiple facets of life, gives rise to a host of future developments as well as problems in the sphere of information security. As time progresses, we have to brace ourselves for more attacks that have the potential to cripple the security of our information assets and infostructures.

One of the most important tendencies is the advancement of cyber threats as a result of AI and machine learning advancements. The possibility of AI-enabled attacks immediately raises concerns about how efficiently and precisely criminals will now commit such attacks (Fantin et al., 2020). The circumstances in which these abnormal transformations occur necessitate better defensive actions and fresh strategies that are flexible to the novel transformation techniques.

Moreover, the massive penetration of IoT devices increases the target area and, consequently, the need for a holistic strategy to safeguard networks and systems. The increasing number of smart devices constitutes new entry points for cybercriminals, thereby necessitating the need for stringent policies aimed at security provisions (Fantin et al., 2020).

Furthermore, the development of quantum computers could potentially jeopardize the existing system of encryption, and therefore, cryptographic systems must withstand quantum threats urgently. However, the biggest worry today is the prospective failure of these systems to withstand the quantum while countries and their firms are racing to apply quantum technology.

The growing interdependence of nation-states and their economies and the proliferation of cyber-physical systems create additional challenges for the already complex issue of cyber security. Key sectors—such as energy, transportation, and healthcare—are becoming increasingly dependent on interconnected systems; hence, there is a need to defend against the damaging effects of potential cyber and cyber-physical (Renaud et al., 2019).

In tandem with the evolution of cryptography and information systems security, it is vital that concerns linked to personal security, data rights, and ethics also receive significant attention. Legislative directions regarding collecting, storing, and using personal and sensitive information will be crucial to the cybersecurity of the future. In addressing such complex problems, a holistic approach is needed to reinforce the improvement of technology with appropriate policy positions and foster collaboration across industries and countries.

Building active measures in advance—the exchange of threat information, continuous employee training, and cost-effectiveness—will be important for strengthening global cyber security. To summarize, with the integration of new technologies, alteration of threat scenarios, and change in geopolitical situations, the cybersecurity industry needs to be more focused on enjoying dynamic development along with simple strategy formulation.

Recommendations for Strengthening Global Cyber Policies

Countries must prioritize collaborative efforts to tackle evolving cyber threats and strengthen global cybersecurity. Establishing a global cybersecurity organization, as suggested by Biden et al. (2023), would provide a centralized platform for facilitating information sharing, setting international security standards, and coordinating responses among member nations. This initiative could include joint cyber defense exercises and knowledge exchange to enhance collective cyber resilience.

Transparency and accountability are essential for building trust and strengthening cyberspace. Governments can play a significant role by openly reporting cyber incidents and sharing threat intelligence, which would increase global awareness and help detect recurring attack patterns (Lunati et al., 2023). Simultaneously, fostering strong public-private partnerships (PPPs) is crucial for innovation and the dissemination of effective cybersecurity practices (Biden et al., 2023).

Embedding cybersecurity education and awareness initiatives into school curricula and professional training programs is another critical step toward societal resilience. Training individuals to recognize and mitigate cyber risks empowers communities to better defend against cyber threats (Lunati et al., 2023).

Adherence to international cybersecurity norms and guidelines must also be a priority. Aligning national policies with treaties like the Budapest Convention or frameworks like the Tallinn Manual can harmonize legal approaches to cybercrime and enhance international coordination in responding to threats (Lunati et al., 2023).

Countries must also improve mechanisms for attributing cyberattacks to deter malicious cyber activities. This would enable effective legal action against perpetrators while discouraging harmful behavior. Investment in the research and development of advanced cybersecurity technologies, such as quantum-resistant encryption and AI-powered threat detection systems, will further bolster defenses against sophisticated cyber threats (Biden et al., 2023).

By implementing these measures, countries can jointly address vulnerabilities, enhance digital resilience, and establish a secure global cyber ecosystem.

References:

- Renaud, Karen, Zimmermann, Verena, 2019, https://core.ac.uk/download/323052064.pdf

- Igonor, Andy, Ikitemur, Gokhan, Karabacak, Bilge, "FUSE (Franklin University Scholarly Exchange)," 2020, https://core.ac.uk/download/386976301.pdf

- Batarseh, Feras A., 2022, http://arxiv.org/abs/2206.09465

- Bauer, Cristen, Chaisse, Julien, "Scholarship@Vanderbilt Law", 2019, https://core.ac.uk/download/479062323.pdf

- Biden, Joseph R., "DigitalCommons@University of Nebraska - Lincoln," 2023, https://core.ac.uk/download/590237239.pdf

- Fantin, Stephano, Ferreira, Afonso, Pupillo, Lorenzo, 2020, https://core.ac.uk/download/287647893.pdf

- Radanliev, Petar, "Springer Nature", 2024, https://core.ac.uk/download/598036338.pdf

- Adam C. Gastineau, Adam Henschke, Levi J. West, Mick Keelty, Nicholas G. Evans, Shannon B. Ford, "National Security College (ANU)", 2024, https://core.ac.uk/download/pdf/30674373.pdf

- Arcuri, Maria Cristina, Brogi, Marina, Gandolfi, Gino, "'Virtus Interpress'", 2018, https://core.ac.uk/download/154948114.pdf

- Klee Aiken, "Australian Strategic Policy Institute," 2024, https://core.ac.uk/download/pdf/30675091.pdf

- Zhang, Michelle, "' The Ohio State University Libraries", 2020, https://core.ac.uk/download/305123572.pdf

- Jess Woodall, Klee Aiken, Tobias Feakin, "Australian Strategic Policy Institute," 2024, https://core.ac.uk/download/pdf/30674827.pdf

- Inter-American Development Bank, "FIU Digital Commons," 2016, https://core.ac.uk/download/429962850.pdf

- Lunati, Mia, "ODU Digital Commons," 2023, https://core.ac.uk/download/595866316.pdf

- Mobilio, Sarah B., "Monterey, CA; Naval Postgraduate School," 2024, https://core.ac.uk/download/618458516.pdf

7

EMERGING TECHNOLOGIES: AI, QUANTUM COMPUTING, AND BIOTECHNOLOGY

Novel Technological Paradigms

IN THE KALEIDOSCOPIC MAELSTROM of technological evolution, quantum leaps, and paradigm-shattering innovations relentlessly reshape our sociopolitical tapestry (Singh et al., 2024; Radanliev et al., 2024). The inexorable march of artificial intelligence, quantum computing's mystifying potential, and biotechnology's transformative prowess catalyze unprecedented metamorphoses in human civilization's fabric (Batarseh et al., 2022; Bauer et al., 2019).

These technological tsunamis ripple through economic ecosystems, fracturing traditional power structures while birthing novel socioeconomic paradigms (Hellmeier et al., 2023). In this labyrinthine dance of innovation, governments grapple with Prometheus's fire – attempting to harness its transformative energy while containing its potentially devastating consequences (McCarthy et al., 2019). The digital renaissance spawns thorny ethical dilemmas, byzantine regulatory challenges, and kaleidoscopic opportunities that defy conventional governance frameworks (Kettemann et al., 2020).

Within this crucible of change, the intricate web of emerging technologies demands sophisticated orchestration across borders, cultures, and ideologies (Burri et al., 2022). Innovation ecosystems flourish in this fertile chaos, where cross-pollination between disciplines yields unexpected breakthroughs and paradigm shifts (Zhang et al., 2020). Yet, this technological cornucopia also breeds vulnerabilities – digital panopticons, algorithmic bias, and cyber warfare lurking in the shadows of progress (Elbe et al., 2021).

As we navigate this techno-social labyrinth, the imperative for nuanced understanding grows exponentially (West et al., 2018). The convergence of disparate technological streams creates synergistic phenomena that challenge traditional analytical frameworks (Arcuri et al., 2018). This technological zeitgeist demands a holistic appreciation of its multifaceted implications, from quantum encryption's cryptographic revolution to AI's cognitive augmentation of human capability (Fantin et al., 2020; Bajwa et al., 2021).

Artificial Intelligence: Disruptive Potential and Policy Ramifications

Artificial Intelligence's transformative tendrils reach deep into the fabric of modern society, unleashing unprecedented disruption across healthcare's hallowed halls, finance's volatile markets, and defense's strategic bastions. This technological tsunami brings both dazzling possibilities and thorny predicaments, demanding nimble policy frameworks from governments and international bodies grappling with AI's relentless march.

In medicine, AI algorithms dance through vast data constellations, unveiling hidden diagnostic patterns and crafting bespoke treatment symphonies while accelerating drug discovery's typically glacial pace. Yet this digital revolution breeds thorny ethical dilemmas—patient data sanctity hangs precariously, while AI's potential biases lurk like digital specters, demanding robust regulatory architectures and stringent industry protocols.

Financial markets writhe under AI's algorithmic grip as machine learning revolutionizes everything from lightning-fast trading to fraud detection's eternal vigilance. Customer experiences morph through AI's predictive alchemy, yet this transformation spawns murky questions about algorithmic accountability and traditional employment's uncertain fate in this brave new world.

The military sphere trembles as AI rewrites ancient strategic doctrines. Autonomous weapons systems emerge from digital forges, while predictive analytics illuminate conflict's foggy horizons. However, ethical quandaries multiply like hydra heads - from AI-powered warfare's moral maze to cybersecurity's endless cat-and-mouse game, where vulnerabilities could trigger catastrophic cascade effects.

Global governance frameworks struggle to keep pace with AI's quantum leaps, necessitating unprecedented international coordination. Multi-stakeholder dialogues must navigate treacherous waters between innovation's siren song and ethical imperatives while crafting policies that transcend national boundaries.

This technological revolution demands delicate calibration between progress and prudence. Success hinges on orchestrating a complex dance between policymakers' foresight, industry's dynamism, and the global community's collective wisdom, ensuring AI's bounty serves humanity's greater good while avoiding its darker potentials.

AI's Influence on Healthcare, Finance, and Defense

Artificial Intelligence is becoming a major player in various fields, changing how we engage with healthcare, finance, and defense. In healthcare, AI advancements are changing how we diagnose diseases, create treatment plans, and personalize medical care. AI systems can look at complex medical data to spot trends and make accurate predictions, which helps in early disease detection and improving patient care (Brown et al., 2022). Additionally, AI-enabled robotic tools support doctors in carrying out complicated surgeries, which minimizes mistakes and improves surgical results. Integrating AI in healthcare could lower medical costs, increase service access, and ultimately save lives.

In finance, AI systems are used for predictions, spotting fraud, and algorithmic trading. Machine learning methods process large financial data sets quickly and accurately, allowing financial companies to identify market patterns, assess risks, and improve investment strategies. Furthermore, AI-powered chatbots and virtual assistants enhance customer service by offering customized suggestions and streamlining regular banking tasks (Sindiramutty et al., 2023). The role of AI in protecting financial organizations is growing more important, as it continuously monitors and recognizes possible security threats to safeguard sensitive information and transactions.

In the defense sector, AI technologies are changing military operations, gathering intelligence, and planning strategies. Drones and unmanned aerial vehicles powered by AI carry out surveillance, identify targets, and analyze situations with high accuracy and efficiency. In addition, AI-based predictive analytics help military planners foresee potential threats, allocate resources more effectively and create responsive strategies (Brown et al., 2022).

AI also strengthens cybersecurity by automatically detecting and addressing cyber threats, thus protecting important infrastructure and maintaining national security.

However, the rise of AI in defense raises worries about autonomous warfare and the ethical issues surrounding AI-run military actions, which require careful consideration of international laws and standards. AI's significant influence on healthcare, finance, and defense is substantial, changing operational practices and decision-making in these key fields. As AI evolves, policymakers, industry experts, and researchers need to work together to tackle ethical, legal, and societal concerns while fully utilizing AI's potential to improve human well-being, stimulate economic development, and enhance global security.

Quantum Computing: A Paradigm Shift in Computational Capability

Quantum computing is a big change in computing ideas and communication methods, offering strong processing power and the chance to change many fields. Unlike traditional computers that use binary bits, quantum computers work with quantum bits or qubits, which can be in many states simultaneously due to quantum superposition and entanglement principles (AKHTAR et al., 2024). This key difference allows quantum computers to perform complicated calculations much faster than classical computers, especially for large data analysis, optimization problems, and cryptography tasks (Sindiramutty et al., 2023).

The effects of this change are wide-ranging. In scientific research, quantum computing can speed up drug development, improve molecular modeling, and solve complex physics problems that traditional methods struggle with. In finance, companies can gain significant advantages from quantum computing's ability to handle complex risk assessments, refine portfolios, and carry out rapid algorithmic trading, potentially changing financial markets (Sindiramutty et al., 2023).

Additionally, cybersecurity is facing a major change, as quantum computing can improve encryption methods and challenge current security systems. The impact of quantum computing also includes telecommunications and data sharing, with techniques like quantum key distribution paving the way for new secure communication options (AKHTAR et al., 2024).

As organizations and industries grow eager to harness quantum computing's potential, the importance of funding research and development to improve hardware, software, and algorithms is clear. However, along with its great promise, quantum computing presents serious challenges, including technical difficulties in keeping qubits stable, correcting errors, and reducing environmental noise. Ethical issues about how quantum computing impacts privacy and national security also need careful discussion and international cooperation (Sindiramutty et al., 2023).

At the junction of technology, policy, and global relations, the rise of quantum computing requires solid governance to understand its social, economic, and geopolitical effects. In the end, quantum computing is not just a tech breakthrough; it's also a chance for global teamwork and strategic planning as we face the challenges of a more quantum-influenced world.

Quantum Cryptography: Ensuring the Security of Future Communications

Regarding cryptographic evolution, quantum cryptography emerges as an enigmatic paradigm shift, transcending conventional security paradigms through its unprecedented manipulation of quantum mechanical principles. This revolutionary methodology, far from being merely incremental, represents a quantum leap in securing our increasingly vulnerable digital cosmos (Aboy et al., 2023).

The arcane intersection of quantum phenomena—entanglement's "spooky action at distance" and superposition's paradoxical duality—engenders an intrinsically secure communication framework where the mere act of observation catalyzes irreversible perturbations in the quantum state. This phenomenological safeguard transcends traditional cryptographic boundaries, manifesting an almost metaphysical layer of protection that renders conventional cryptanalysis obsolete.

The transformative implications of quantum cryptographic systems reverberate across multifarious domains—from clandestine governmental communique to quotidian financial transactions—while simultaneously presenting labyrinthine technical challenges that demand innovative solutions (University of Office M of the President V for Research and Dean of the School G, 2021). The implementation of quantum key distribution (QKD) systems grapples with byzantine complexities: quantum decoherence, environmental perturbations, and the intricate choreography of standardization across heterogeneous networks.

Beyond the technical realm, quantum cryptography catalyzes profound sociopolitical tensions, particularly in the delicate balance between privacy preservation and national security imperatives. The technology's potential to create impenetrable communication channels raises provocative questions about surveillance, sovereignty, and the evolving nature of digital governance in an increasingly quantum-enabled world.

This cryptographic revolution, while fraught with implementation challenges, portends a seismic shift in secure communication paradigms. The inexorable march toward quantum supremacy demands a nuanced, collaborative approach to governance—one that harmonizes technological innovation with ethical considerations while fostering global cooperation in an era where digital security becomes increasingly paramount.

As we navigate this quantum frontier, the technology's transformative potential in reshaping digital diplomacy and international security architectures becomes increasingly apparent. Though the path to widespread quantum cryptographic deployment remains serpentine, its promise of unprecedented security resilience renders it an indispensable cornerstone of our evolving digital ecosystem.

Biotechnology: Progress and Ethical Dilemmas

In an era of unprecedented scientific advancement, biotechnology has emerged, revolutionizing everything from the intricacies of healthcare to the fundamental ways we grow our food and protect our planet. The rippling effects of these breakthroughs have spawned a labyrinth of ethical conundrums that demand our immediate attention and thoughtful regulation (Marianne A Azer et al., 2024).

At the forefront of this biological revolution stands CRISPR-Cas9, a game-changing gene-editing tool. Like a molecular sculptor, it promises to chisel away inherited diseases with unprecedented precision. Yet this power to rewrite the very code of life raises thorny questions: Where do we draw the line? How far should we venture into the depths of human genetic modification? (Jeyaraman N et al., 2024)

GMOs have transformed agriculture forever. These engineered crops, resilient and abundant, feed millions. But concerns linger. Environmental impacts remain unclear. Health implications spark fierce debate. We need smart, balanced regulations - now.
Meanwhile, in a fascinating convergence of silicon and cells, bioinformatics has emerged. This marriage of biotechnology and computing processes vast amounts of biological data, accelerating drug discovery and personalizing medicine. Yet this digital revolution in biotechnology isn't without its shadows - privacy concerns loom large, consent issues multiply, and the specter of genetic data misuse haunts progress (Marianne A Azer et al., 2024).

As we push the boundaries of what's possible, a critical question emerges: Who benefits? Biotechnological breakthroughs must not become luxuries for the few. Social inequities yawn wide. The technology gap between nations deepens. We must act decisively to ensure fair access to these life-changing innovations (Jeyaraman N et al., 2024).

The path forward is dialogue, collaboration, and action. Bioethicists must speak with scientists, policymakers, and the public. Only through this complex dance of perspectives can we forge ethical frameworks that both protect and promote progress. The future of biotechnology hangs in the balance—brilliant with promise yet fraught with responsibility.

The Convergence of Biotechnology and Information Technology

In a dazzling confluence of scientific domains, biotechnology, and information technology are orchestrating an unprecedented revolution. This marriage of disciplines - once separate universes - now propels humanity into realms of innovation previously confined to science fiction (Sacha et al., 2013). Like a double helix intertwining with binary code, these fields merge to create something extraordinary: a new frontier where living systems meet computational power and where genetic codes dance with algorithms.

Healthcare has transformed. Picture personalized medicine—not as a distant dream but as today's reality. Advanced genetic sequencing, powered by sophisticated algorithms, peers into our molecular makeup with extraordinary precision (Araya D et al., 2022). Diagnostic tools have evolved from clunky machines to elegant wearables that whisper their findings directly to the cloud. The democratization of health technology marches forward, putting powerful genetic insights into everyday hands.

In research laboratories worldwide, supercomputers hum ceaselessly, simulating complex biological systems in mere hours - tasks that once demanded years. Cloud platforms soar above geographical boundaries, enabling scientists across continents to collaborate seamlessly, their shared data flowing through secure digital channels (Sacha et al., 2013). The pace of discovery accelerates, driven by this powerful synthesis of biological insight and computational might.

Artificial intelligence emerges as a game-changer. Machine learning algorithms sift through vast oceans of biological data, spotting patterns invisible to human eyes. In agriculture, this technological symphony orchestrates a revolution: smart sensors probe soil conditions, satellites track crop health, and predictive analytics optimize every aspect of farming. The result? A more sustainable, precise approach to feeding our growing world.

Yet this scientific renaissance extends far beyond conventional boundaries. In laboratories and research centers, scientists engineer crops that laugh in the face of climate change, while synthetic biology pioneers craft solutions for environmental remediation. Bio-based materials emerge with properties that seem to defy nature, their development guided by computational models of unprecedented sophistication.

However, this powerful partnership walks a tightrope. The ethical implications loom large, particularly in gene editing and genetic engineering. We need robust governance frameworks, not just guidelines scribbled in the margins (Araya D et al., 2022). Data privacy concerns cast long shadows: How do we protect the most intimate details of our genetic makeup in an increasingly connected world?

The path forward demands global cooperation. We need voices from every corner of society—scientists, ethicists, policymakers, and citizens—engaged in meaningful dialogue about these transformative technologies. The stakes couldn't be higher: We're not just shaping tools and techniques; we're crafting the future itself.

As this technological convergence accelerates, we stand at a crossroads. The potential for breakthrough solutions to humanity's greatest challenges beckons, but realizing this potential requires wisdom, foresight, and an unwavering commitment to ethical progress. In this dance between biotechnology and information technology, every step must be choreographed with precision, and every movement must be guided by the compass of human values and societal benefit.

Global Standards and Regulatory Challenges

The convergence of revolutionary technologies - AI, quantum computing, and biotechnology - into global markets heralds an unprecedented transformation, unleashing a labyrinthine web of regulatory challenges that defy conventional governance frameworks. This technological renaissance, while promising extraordinary advances, demands an intricate choreography of international cooperation to navigate the regulatory maze and establish coherent global standards (University of Office M of the President V for Research and Dean of the School G, 2021). As our world grows increasingly interconnected, the imperative for unified frameworks becomes not just crucial but existential in orchestrating these innovations while preserving ethical integrity and fortifying security measures.

The architectural challenge of constructing global standards emerges as a Herculean task, necessitating the harmonization of disparate regulatory ecosystems, cultural paradigms, and juridical frameworks that vary dramatically across geographical boundaries. These standards must perform an elaborate balancing act - nurturing innovation's flame while erecting robust safeguards against potential risks. The synchronization of regulatory approaches transcends mere preference; it represents a fundamental necessity. This alignment catalyzes interoperability, cultivates trust, and creates fertile ground for scientific and technological cross-pollination. Yet, bridging these multifaceted differences demands intensive diplomatic finesse and consensus-building among an intricate network of policymakers, regulatory authorities, and cultural stakeholders on the global stage (University of Office M of the President V for Research and Dean of the School G, 2021).

The breakneck velocity of technological evolution poses a formidable challenge to conventional regulatory mechanisms, which frequently struggle to maintain pace. AI's meteoric rise, for instance, introduces urgent concerns regarding privacy infractions, algorithmic prejudice, and accountability frameworks. These challenges routinely outstrip the implementation of adequate oversight measures. Similarly, quantum computing's unprecedented computational capabilities and biotechnology's potential to fundamentally alter biological systems present labyrinthine ethical quandaries and security considerations, demanding dynamic regulatory responses capable of addressing far-reaching implications.

The increasing convergence of these transformative technologies amplifies the urgency for comprehensive global regulatory frameworks. The synthesis of AI with biotechnology or quantum computing introduces unprecedented complexities that conventional regulatory approaches struggle to address. To remain relevant, regulatory mechanisms must exhibit extraordinary adaptability, evolving in lockstep with technological advancement. Simultaneously, the intricate web of global economic interdependence necessitates regulatory frameworks that deftly navigate international commerce, cross-border collaboration, and economic symbiosis. Economic factors - including investment patterns, intellectual property frameworks, and technology transfer agreements - are inextricably linked to the dissemination and commercialization of emerging technologies in fiercely competitive global marketplaces.

Consequently, effective regulatory strategies must meticulously consider their cascading effects on market dynamics, trade relationships, and international collaborations. Policymakers confront the delicate challenge of fostering innovation and economic vitality while steadfastly upholding ethical principles and societal values. This equilibrium demands sustained, multilateral dialogue among diverse stakeholders, encompassing governmental bodies, corporate entities, academic institutions, and civil society organizations, ensuring equitable and inclusive technological regulation.

A critical consideration in this landscape is the potential pitfall of excessive regulation or regional inconsistencies. Overly restrictive measures risk suffocating innovation by creating insurmountable barriers for entrepreneurs, startups, and research initiatives while impeding the global proliferation of transformative technologies. Rigid intellectual property regimes, for instance, might restrict access to vital technologies in developing regions, exacerbating global disparities. Addressing these challenges requires international coordination and adaptive policy frameworks that accommodate diverse market conditions and societal needs (Aboy et al., 2023). Collaborative mechanisms must vigilantly guard against regulatory fragmentation, which could precipitate inefficiencies and impede progress.

The international community must ultimately forge ahead toward a cohesive, inclusive regulatory ecosystem that prioritizes ethical responsibility and technological safety without compromising innovative potential. Policymakers must acknowledge the intricate interplay between technology, commerce, and society in addressing regulatory challenges, ensuring equitable access to emerging technologies while mitigating associated risks. Through sustained collaboration and strategic foresight, we can chart a course for AI, quantum computing, and biotechnology that maximizes their transformative potential while fostering economic growth and societal advancement. This delicate equilibrium hinges on coordinated action that aligns technological progress with humanity's enduring aspirations.

Impact on International Trade and Economic Development

The technological revolution spearheaded by AI, quantum computing, and biotechnology is orchestrating a profound metamorphosis in global commerce and economic trajectories. These disruptive innovations are catalyzing unprecedented transformations across industrial landscapes while fundamentally recalibrating the dynamics of international business paradigms.

In global trade, these technologies are architecting sophisticated supply chain networks, revolutionizing logistics frameworks, and deploying prescient market analytics. AI-driven algorithms are orchestrating intricate inventory management systems, decoding demand patterns, and revolutionizing customer relationship matrices, thereby amplifying cross-border trade efficiencies exponentially (Boyd et al., 2020). Concurrently, biotechnological breakthroughs have engineered genetically optimized crops, manifesting enhanced yield potentials and pest resistance capabilities, thus reconfiguring agricultural trade dynamics and fortifying global food security architectures (Harfouche et al., 2023).

Quantum computing emerges as a transformative force in data security paradigms and communication encryption protocols - foundational pillars of international trade and financial systems. Its unparalleled computational prowess offers revolutionary solutions to cybersecurity vulnerabilities, fostering enhanced trust in digital transaction ecosystems (Boyd et al., 2020).

These technological innovations are reshaping the economic growth landscape, spawning entrepreneurial ecosystems and vibrant innovation hubs globally. Tech-centric startups leveraging AI, quantum computing, and biotechnology are emerging as powerful economic catalysts, attracting international capital flows and facilitating economic diversification.

Nevertheless, the asymmetric distribution of technological access presents a critical challenge, potentially exacerbating existing trade disparities and economic schisms. Developing economies face significant hurdles in technological adaptation, risking further marginalization in the global economic order. This underscores the imperative for robust international collaboration and knowledge dissemination frameworks through strategic technology transfer initiatives (Harfouche et al., 2023).

The transformative impact of these technological paradigms on global trade and economic development necessitates proactive policy frameworks, strategic partnerships, and capacity-building initiatives to optimize innovation potential while ensuring equitable access and benefit distribution across the global community.

Future Directions and Strategic Recommendations

In the crucible of our technological zeitgeist, where silicon dreams interweave with quantum possibilities, a labyrinthine tapestry of diplomatic imperatives emerges, demanding unprecedented orchestration of global will. The kaleidoscopic convergence of nations must forge an architectural framework—a digital Magna Carta—that harmonizes the discordant symphony of emerging technologies (Commission NS on Intelligence A (US), 2020).

Within this maelstrom of innovation, investment becomes the lodestone of progress, magnetizing resources toward the triumvirate of AI, quantum computing, and biotechnology. This pecuniary devotion must transcend mere capital infusion, spawning intellectual ecosystems where the cross-pollination of disciplines births revelatory insights. The crystal ball of strategic foresight, wielded with prescient precision, becomes our navigational compass through these tempestuous waters of change.

The amalgamation of disparate technological streams creates a confluence of possibility—where quantum algorithms dance with biological imperatives, and artificial intelligence weaves through supply chains with serpentine grace (Boyd et al., 2020). This technological fusion demands a renaissance in research methodology, where disciplinary boundaries dissolve like morning mist before the dawn of innovation.

Ethical considerations must serve as the North Star in this journey, illuminating the path toward human-centric technological evolution (Commission NS on Intelligence A (US), 2020). The marriage of public ingenuity with private enterprise creates a crucible of collaboration, forging solutions that transcend traditional boundaries. This symbiotic partnership must navigate the treacherous waters between innovation and equity, ensuring technological bounty doesn't become the exclusive province of the privileged few (Harfouche et al., 2023).

As we venture forth into this brave new world, our technological odyssey must be guided by the twin stars of ethical stewardship and collaborative governance. Only through this delicate balance can we ensure that the fruits of innovation nourish the entire global garden rather than just its most privileged corners.

References:

- Sacha, Gómez Moñivas, Varona, Pablo, "'IOP Publishing'", 2013, https://repositorio.uam.es/bitstream/handle/10486/665596/artificial_sacha_NT_2013_ps.pdf?sequence=1

- Daniel Araya, Meg King, "Centre for International Governance Innovation (CIGI)," 2022, https://core.ac.uk/download/539980921.pdf

- Harfouche, Antoine, Nakhle, Farid, "CREA Forestry and Wood", 2023, https://core.ac.uk/download/553286973.pdf

- Boyd, Matt, Wilson, Nick, "Institute for Governance and Policy Studies & the School of Government," 2020, https://core.ac.uk/download/560330773.pdf

- AKHTAR, Zarif Bin, TAJBIUL RAWOL, Ahmed, "Journal of Information Sciences," 2024, https://core.ac.uk/download/618381966.pdf

- Sindiramutty, Siva Raja, 2023, http://arxiv.org/abs/2401.00286

- National Security Commission on Artificial Intelligence (U.S.), "National Security Commission on Artificial Intelligence (U.S.)", 2020, https://core.ac.uk/download/482295821.pdf

- Aboy, Mateo, Brongersma, Mark, Cohen, I. Glenn, De Jong, Eline, Floridi, Luciano, Gasser, Urs, Kop, Mauritz,

Laflamme, Raymond, Minssen, Timo, Quintel, Teresa, 2023, http://arxiv.org/abs/2303.16671

- University of Maine Office of the Vice President for Research and Dean of the Graduate School, "DigitalCommons@UMaine," 2021, https://core.ac.uk/download/482033909.pdf

- Brown, Jason C, Carrott, James, Johnson, Brian David, Lindsay, Greg, Vanatta, Natalie, "USMA Digital Commons," 2022, https://core.ac.uk/download/542863029.pdf

- Marianne A. Azer, Rasha Samir, "International Journal of Advanced Computer Science and Applications," Volume(Vol. 15, No. 7), 2024, http://saiconferences.com/Downloads/Volume15No7/Paper_142-Overview_of_the_Complex_Landscape_and_Future_Directions_of_Ethics.pdf

- Naveen Jeyaraman, Madhan Jeyaraman, Sankalp Yadav, Swaminathan Ramasubramanian, Sangeetha Balaji, "Cureus," Volume(Vol 16, Issue 8), e67486, 2024, https://www.cureus.com/articles/278342-revolutionizing-healthcare-the-emerging-role-of-quantum-computing-in-enhancing-medical-technology-and-treatment.pdf

8

THE TECHNOLOGICAL ARMS RACE AND GLOBAL POWER DYNAMICS

The Technological Arms Race

In today's high-stakes technological battlefield, an intricate dance of power unfolds between nation-states and corporate behemoths. Gone are the simple Cold War dynamics; welcome to a multi-dimensional chess game where traditional boundaries blur and new players emerge with surprising frequency.

The United States, long comfortable in its role as the world's tech heavyweight, finds itself in an unprecedented position. While Silicon Valley continues to pump out groundbreaking innovations in artificial intelligence and quantum computing, it's no longer the unchallenged champion it once was (Horowitz et al., 2018). Think of it as a seasoned boxer suddenly finding themselves surrounded by hungry newcomers in an expanded ring.

Enter China - the dragon that's not just breathing fire but systematically building a technological empire. Through ambitious initiatives like Made in China 2025 and the Belt and Road Initiative, Beijing isn't just catching up; it's charting its own course to tech supremacy (Lungu et al., 2005). With state coffers backing everything from semiconductor development to artificial intelligence research, China's approach combines strategic patience with explosive bursts of innovation.

Russia, meanwhile, plays a fascinating game of asymmetric warfare. Rather than competing across all technological fronts, it has carved out specialized niches in cybersecurity and military technology. Like a master chess player, Russia focuses on specific pieces rather than controlling the entire board.

The European Union presents yet another fascinating dynamic - imagine 27 countries trying to coordinate their technological orchestra while each maintains its own unique rhythm. Their collaborative approach, though sometimes cumbersome, brings together diverse expertise while grappling with thorny ethical questions that other players might conveniently ignore.

But here's where it gets really interesting: smaller nations have found ways to punch well above their weight class. Israel, with its bustling startup ecosystem, has become a cybersecurity powerhouse. South Korea dominates in telecommunications, while India's software engineering prowess makes it an indispensable player in the global tech landscape.

Perhaps most intriguingly, corporate titans like Google, Amazon, and Microsoft have emerged as quasi-sovereign entities in this technological grand game. These companies, with budgets rivaling small nations and user bases exceeding the population of most countries, blur the traditional lines between corporate and national interests. Their research labs often outpace government initiatives, while their global reach challenges traditional notions of national sovereignty.

The result? A fascinating ecosystem where power dynamics shift as rapidly as the technology itself evolves. Traditional allies might find themselves competing in certain domains while collaborating in others. Corporate giants might simultaneously partner with and challenge government initiatives. It's a complex web where innovation, ambition, and strategic necessity create unexpected alliances and rivalries.

This isn't just about who has the biggest research budget or the most patents. It's about who can adapt fastest, innovate smartest, and navigate the increasingly complex intersection of technology, geopolitics, and economic power. As these players continue their intricate dance, the very nature of global influence and power continues to be redefined.

Global Hegemony and Technological Dominance

The turn of the 21st century saw a global power race that emphasized being technologically advanced as the main goal. Nations and businesses are trying to dominate the creation, use, and management of emerging technologies as they understand the reputational implications for their standing within the globe. A significant part of this understanding is the realization that being in possession of the highest-grade technology enables one to exercise strong influence over the world's politics, economy, and security as a whole (Horowitz et al., 2018). Technological advancement is a key aspect in strengthening a nation's traditional military powers, as well as augmenting its capabilities in cyberspace activities, space operations, and information conflicts. The capacity to innovate and use newer technologies in warfare and strategic matters is altering the existing balance of power and the prevailing notions about deterrence and influence (Lee S, 2015). Furthermore, it has a strong impact on how a state is perceived in terms of competence and leadership with regard to its influence and diplomatic resources in the international environment. Countries that are well-equipped with advanced technologies are granted more visibility to international issues and, as such, are able to redefine the norms and procedures that govern the proliferation and usage of these technologies.

Consequently, there is a clear relationship between a nation's technological superiority and its economic strength that influences trade relations, aid, and availability of vital inputs. It acts as the cornerstone of the nation's might and its ability to compete by placing it in the midst of new ideas and industrialization as well. Furthermore, the relationship between the improvement of technologies and the power of the nation doesn't concern only state organs but also transnational corporations and organizations that have a considerable impact on the world of technology. Their capital, research papers, and authority in the market promote technologies and influence the relationship of forces in the world. Therefore, integrating technology with power is not easy and time-consuming. The type of problems that accompany this combination requires a long, detailed analysis. As different states strive for dominance in new technologies and seek to apply them in political struggles, the danger of conflict and confrontation increases. Therefore, to avoid a conflict-inducing arms race while ensuring the benefits of technological advances contribute to global equilibrium and safety, an equilibrium between rivalry and partnership must be established.

Military Applications of Emerging Technologies

The technological evolution throughout this century has redefined military capabilities and strategies, which, in turn, has considerably altered modern warfare. There is a greater reliance on advanced technologies to improve the global perceptions of countries and their militaries. Modern technologies have widened the military scope, ranging from the use of unmanned systems to advanced cyber tools and artificial intelligence (Horowitz et al.,

2018). There is a possibility and high certainty factors that the dynamics of warfare will change with the integration of AI, considering that the tasks of decision-making, responsibilities, and physical involvement of individuals in the battles will be increased. Autonomous weapon systems with AI support may have advantages, but issues regarding ethical inquiry remain problematic, mainly because of the ability of machines to make kill decisions (Viviano et al., 2022). Furthermore, employing AI in military intelligence, surveillance, and reconnaissance systems can potentially alter reconciled and analyzed information and enhance response mechanisms. These results in lower risk to military personnel and quick, low-cost, effective monitoring and striking capabilities. Attack drones assist extensively and are now a vital part of any army's arsenal, providing superior intelligence, aid, and drone attacks in modern combat missions. The developments in swarm technology also permit the integrated combat of multiple drones for stronger combat tactics.

Chinese cyber capabilities have fundamentally altered the nature of warfare, with the importance and reach of cyberspace having significantly risen to the point where the military's cyber units and institutions are central to military strategy and vice versa. The proliferation of information technology, advanced forms of malware, and political warfare meant campaigns proliferated in entirely new surroundings, expanding, transforming, and potentially revolutionizing the character of conflict and national security concerns. Space Cyber security has increasingly become 'less of a nice to have and more of a must have' while also been trained to be integrated into core 'spaces', which will start to shape how countries view the importance of cyberspace. The rise of biotechnology means new questions arise, such as what the bioweapon theory is, whether it is about personalistic-looking soldiers with augmented abilities or controlled genetic soldiers. As the bioweapons concept, with its necropolitical goals, merges with Biodefense, this opens up some troubling moral and legal questions that would need to be resolved, which means a careful look, as well as international executions, would be needed to help retain the state virtue or altruism. The phenomenal pace of development of advanced systems of sight, sound, touch, and smell sensors, as well as manipulating them, has and is impacting every physical and virtual interaction, allowing the world superpowers to redefine militarism even further.

Economic Aspects of Advanced Technology

The rapid spread and adoption of emerging technologies have profound implications for the economies of different sectors and countries. Most countries allocate a lot of resources to the R&D and application of new technologies because they want a competitive edge in technology on a global scale (Lee S, 2015). This quest to be the best in technology not only determines the geopolitical standing of the country but also determines its economic topology. The increase in advanced technologies is also associated with a higher level of productivity and efficiency in different industries. Incorporating technology such as automation, artificial intelligence, and data mining into business functions can streamline operations, cut costs, and boost output (Lee S, 2015). Thus, it is reasonable to assume that nations that are technologically advanced and innovative will experience increased efficiency, and, most significantly, they will have heightened competitiveness, thus prompting a shift in economic power globally.

Moreover, pouring funds into new technologies and tools assists in the formation of new economies and jobs. The nurturing of active environments centered on new technologies creates jobs in skilled areas such as engineering, software development, and data science. These innovations can also stimulate new businesses and start-up companies, encouraging more productive forces and new approaches. However, for the policymakers, it is also critical to address potential issues such as loss of employment and ensure that technological progress ensures inclusive development.

Furthermore, the impact of the economy will affect imports and exports as well as international relations. Countries with better technological know-how often use them as their strong virtues in international trade. Selling complex technologies and the associated services becomes an important part of their trade profiles. Together, these have a profound impact on the global trading system and economic relations. However, how economic goals and technological know-how interact also leads to intricate diplomatic and geopolitical relations and how countries engage in diplomacy and competition therein.

On the other hand, the pursuit of advanced technologies also poses some problems and risks. The development of technologies itself is expensive, and it needs huge funding and resources, which can exert economic strain on governments and firms (Horowitz et al., 2018). Also, the concerns of IPR, cybersecurity, and ethics create further complications for the economics of technological development. For a full understanding of the economic effects of advanced technological development, the participants are required to strike a balance between risk coverage and the promotion of creativity and innovation. As technology develops, economic policies, investment strategies, and international collaborations play an important role in determining economic development. It is also important that advanced technologies, along with their possibilities for and risks to the economy, have equitable outcomes and do not produce adverse consequences while providing economic development that is environmentally sustainable and leaves nobody behind.

Economic Implications of Advanced Technology Development

The technical advances and their applications have strong economic implications for specific sectors and nations. Nations put a good deal of effort into studying, developing, and applying new technologies in the race as it is a technological race (Lee S, 2015). Notably, this race for technological supremacy also changes the strategic position a nation has on the globe! The structure of the economy is also greatly affected. Advancements in technologies cut across improved production and efficiency in many areas. The integration of automation, AI, and data analytics in business activity can enhance processes, reduce costs, and boost production levels (Lee S, 2015). Consequently, countries that are at the forefront of technological changes are more likely to experience an upsurge in their economies and a stronger competitive edge that may have far-reaching alterations to the global economic scenario.

Moreover, focusing on high technology is known to expand new industries and create jobs as well. This way, new active environments oriented toward advanced technologies create workplaces in professional areas such as engineering, software engineering, and data science. These improvements can also stimulate the emergence of new companies and small businesses and innovations. However, it is important for policymakers to address potential issues such as displacement and ensure that technology development results in equitable growth.

In addition to that, the Specifics of the economy and the expenditures resulting from the trade affect international relations. Technologically advanced nations tend to use the same in the market place as one of the toys.. Selling complex technologies and advanced services has become their trade profile, and this alters the trade profile and interdependence across the globe in a significant way. At the same time, the merging of economic imperatives and technology skills provides a number of partnerships and rivalries that are sources of diplomacy and geo-political interactions at the global level.

The need to push the limits of technology is at the same time a prospect and a risk. Researching and enhancing technologies would be extremely capital-intensive, thus straining most governments and business organizations (Horowitz et al., 2018). Additionally, the economic impact of developing technologies is deepened by issues such as the boundaries of intellectual property rights, cyber security, and ethical questions. All the participants have to weigh the need to create new ideas as well as the risks emanating from them and try to appreciate the economic implications of developing advanced technologies. The economic environment is influenced by policy directions, investment strategies, and collaborations since technology is changing. Most importantly, while doing so, the equitable sharing of economic development and negative consequences or risk management becomes crucial in order to be able to harness advanced ideas that lead to growth in sophisticated economies.

Integrative trends and competitive confrontations

Countries should find an equilibrium in the field of information technology that allows them to cooperate and compete simultaneously. The relevance of international cooperation in technology today, arguably, is higher than it has ever been (Lee S, 2015). However, within this effort to collaborate are deep-seated competitive tensions driven by the desire for technological leadership and economic gain (Lee S, 2015). This creates a situation where there is a tug-of-war between the benefits of working together and the pressures of competition.

For one, countries should not disregard the benefits of alliances, diplomacy, and collaboration in the face of global problems, such as the ethical perspective of artificial intelligence, military smart devices, or cybersecurity. These joint efforts can lead to mutual advantages, stimulating innovation and promoting progress on a global scale. On the other hand, the constant need and demand for a competitive advantage drive countries to maximize their investments in companies' technology development and own political objectives and interests instead, making countries pursue conflicting objectives and a geopolitical struggle.

National and state boundaries do not stop these competitive rivalries, which manifest themselves in technological, market, and security-related advances.

Countries are somehow willing to risk everything while competing for dominance in advanced technologies such as artificial intelligence, quantum computing, or biotechnology. What is at risk are breakthroughs that could yield enormous economic and even military gains. The race for talent, IP, or market access provides a lively context where strategy and innovation are fused together.

Furthermore, the interlaced nature of international supply networks and digital marketplaces emphasizes the importance of market power in a technology-centered economy. Countries endeavor to dominate crucial technology standards and infrastructures to control the operating environment and secure a competitive advantage in the international market. These market power pursuits are also intertwined with broader ambitions in the international space since such abilities can bestow one with a global presence.

Still, the fact that there is competition and cooperation in the technology realm provides avenues for expanding the share of strategic centers through forming and joining blocs. These collaborations allow states to enhance their circumventions, mitigate risks, and address shared goals while remaining competitive (Sattar et al., 2023). International partnerships, on the other hand, are complex and must be approached with an open competitive spirit, but they can also provide stability in competitive times if dialogue and trust are prioritized, helping to foster a higher level of security and sustainability in the technological landscape.

In the context of international technology competition, the effective combination of cooperation and competition will have a critical impact on the outcome. This entails having the requisite diplomatic skills, formulating innovative policies, and thoroughly grasping the interplay between global integration and strategic autonomy.

In the end, competition without restraints and international collaboration can provide a foundation for the technologically advanced and robust global community.

Strategic Alliances: A Power Perspective in the Technological Arena

In the rapidly evolving technological world today, the global balance of power relations is shaped strongly by strategic alliances. Countries and large corporations are vying for supremacy in global markets through advanced technologies such as Artificial Intelligence, biotechnology, and quantum computing, and because of this, these partnerships are critical. The general aim of such partnerships is to exploit combined strengths, promote innovation, and deal with the monopolistic tendencies of renowned technological firms (Hagedoorn et al.). Strategic alliances are for the purpose of devolution of power in the face of rapid change in the technology environment so that collaboration occurs, but nationalism is not compromised. As the tech environment is evolving, dynamic evolving partnerships deepen, and they are then able to respond to or take on new tech challenges and opportunities. In this way, these strategic partnerships help nations leverage their resources, knowledge, and technology skills to enhance their global competitiveness. These alliances are not confined to national rivalries but include partnerships between governments, research institutions, and industry players around the world. Leveraging on strengths and minimizing weaknesses, these alliances encourage a collaborative approach to developing technology, thereby enhancing competitiveness globally.

Moreover, these partnerships can help establish norms, rules, and moral values for disruptive technologies in response to the hitherto unbridled growth of invention (Hagedoorn et al). Of course, the formation of strategic collaborations poses challenges, which include factors such as different national agendas, regulatory barriers, intellectual property communication, and data protection. Bringing all the stakeholders' interests into balance would require high diplomacy or mobilization in pursuit of common goals. The delicate balance between trust, transparency, and mutual respect would be hard to strike. Finding the right equilibrium between cooperation and competition in these alliances is imperative because it could prevent the escalation of divisions along the lines of techno-nationalism while allowing for technological development and diffusion at the same time. The choices that are made in the formation and maintenance of these alliances will impact the world in a shift to a more competitive era.

Regulatory and Policy Challenges

The breathtaking speed of new technology has given rise to many rules and policy challenges across continents and countries. Countries are keen on adopting new technologies while managing the associated risks, which indicates an increasing need for strong and robust regulatory frameworks. One key issue is reaching a consensus across countries on regulatory benchmarks.

In international technological governance, the stark disparities between national regulatory frameworks spawn a byzantine web of challenges, particularly in the fields of data protection, cybersecurity, and ethical oversight (Horowitz et al., 2018). These regulatory schisms—far from mere bureaucratic inconveniences—manifest as formidable barriers to seamless cross-border collaboration and technological innovation. While each sovereign nation zealously guards its regulatory autonomy, reflecting deeply entrenched cultural values and strategic imperatives, the imperative for harmonization grows ever more urgent, demanding unprecedented levels of diplomatic finesse and mutual accommodation.

The phenomenon of regulatory lag emerges as a particularly vexing challenge, where the breakneck pace of technological advancement leaves policymakers scrambling to bridge widening governance gaps. This temporal misalignment between innovation and oversight exposes critical vulnerabilities in national security architectures and privacy frameworks, creating a precarious balance between technological progress and societal protection (Horowitz et al., 2018). Legacy regulatory structures, conceived in earlier technological epochs, strain to accommodate the sweeping capabilities and nuanced implications of contemporary innovations, while hasty regulatory responses risk either suffocating innovation or overlooking crucial ethical considerations.

The meteoric rise of artificial intelligence and autonomous systems introduces unprecedented ethical and legal conundrums that transcend traditional jurisdictional boundaries (Erman et al., 2023). These transformative technologies demand novel governance paradigms that can grapple with intricate questions of accountability, algorithmic fairness, and societal impact. The challenge of enforcement looms particularly large in the digital domain, where cyber activities routinely traverse national borders with impunity, necessitating sophisticated international cooperation mechanisms to ensure meaningful compliance and accountability.

A multi-stakeholder approach emerges as the sole viable path forward, demanding intricate orchestration among governmental bodies, institutional frameworks, and private sector entities. This collaborative imperative extends beyond mere regulatory alignment, encompassing knowledge sharing, capacity building, and the establishment of robust international partnerships. The ascendance of technology corporations as quasi-sovereign entities further complicates this landscape, challenging traditional notions of state authority and necessitating innovative approaches to oversight and accountability.

The pursuit of equilibrium between innovation and societal protection demands extraordinary dexterity from policymakers, who must craft regulatory frameworks that simultaneously foster technological advancement and safeguard public interests. This delicate balancing act necessitates an adaptive, forward-looking approach that can anticipate emerging risks while remaining sufficiently flexible to accommodate rapid technological evolution. Success in this endeavor hinges on fostering a global culture of responsible innovation underpinned by shared principles and mutual accountability among all stakeholders in the technological ecosystem.

Future Scenarios and Potential Outcomes

The trajectory of the technological arms race presents a maze of intertwined possibilities, each threading its way into the fabric of global power dynamics, international collaboration, and the moral ambiguities of progress. As innovation accelerates, policymakers, strategists, and scholars alike confront a landscape fraught with profound consequences for humanity. Four distinct scenarios emerge as harbingers of what lies ahead.

Deepening Power Divisions: A Tech-Fueled Geopolitical Rift

The first pathway envisions a world where leading tech powers—nations commanding vast resources and expertise—solidify their dominance, leaving smaller or less advanced countries struggling to catch up. As technological leadership becomes synonymous with geopolitical influence, gaps in power and capability threaten to expand into chasms of destabilization. Consider the ways in which artificial intelligence, cyber innovation, and automation are increasingly shaping economic and military might; the absence of access to these critical tools exacerbates existing inequalities. This "techno-elite" dynamic could fan the flames of global tensions, triggering more hostile economic competition, technology embargoes, or deepened alliance structures tilted heavily toward asymmetric power hierarchies (McFarland et al., 2022).

A Cooperative Horizon: Guiding the Growth of Technology Together

Amid the shadows of division, however, lies a glimmer of possibility: a cooperative global framework that prioritizes shared technological progress rather than ruthless competition. By intertwining governance with ethics and tempering invention with restraint, nations could create alliances built on mutual benefit rather than zero-sum rivalries. In such a vision, international organizations—bolstered by treaties and adaptive policymaking—would establish guardrails for transformative technologies, from AI to bioengineering, ensuring all nations benefit. Collaborative governance would promote transparency, data protection, and security in enduring ways, tempering the risks of reckless innovation while paving the way for a more equitable technological order (Cimpeanu et al., 2022). There is a precedent for such cooperation, though fragile in its success. Reinforcing it requires accountability and trust—commodities increasingly scarce in a world polarized by ambition.

Strategic Realignments: A Redrawing of the Global Map

A third scenario envisions strategic recalculations on a geopolitically fragmented chessboard. As technology emerges as the anchor defining influence, new formations of alignment and competition arise. Countries might forsake traditional loyalties, creating alliances that reflect technological parity, innovation-centric goals, or shared investments in singular advancements like quantum computing or autonomous military systems. These alignments would undermine historical alliances and require countries to rethink their positions in global hierarchies, effectively erasing and redrawing maps of power and cooperation. Importantly, however, such realignments could breed instability as alliances shift unpredictably, forcing nations to shuffle allegiances or risk becoming geopolitical pawns in the tech wars.

A Dark Descent: The Perils of a Military-Centric Tech Race

The most alarming outcome would be a headlong plunge into a military-driven arms race for technological dominance. In this dystopian spiral, innovation is hijacked by militaries seeking an edge in autonomous weaponry, surveillance capabilities, and cyber wars. The regulatory lag that already plagues AI and autonomous systems stands as an existential threat in this context (Horowitz et al., 2018). Without robust oversight, the quest for dominance could yield a cascade of devastating consequences: unregulated drone warfare, AI-driven proxy wars, or catastrophic cyberattacks that devastate critical infrastructure. The ethical void hovering over the development of such tools amplifies their risks, intensifying fears of a future defined by conflict rather than collaboration.

Navigating the Tech Frontier: Steps Toward a Balanced Future

Facing such diverse futures, the onus rests on policymakers, diplomats, and innovators to steer this arms race onto a sustainable path. Active diplomacy rooted in trust and communication remains a lynchpin. Through dialogue and institution-building, competing nations can establish red lines for unacceptable uses of technology while fostering public-private partnerships to drive ethical developments (Erman et al., 2023). Fortifying these efforts requires significant investment in frameworks that bridge technological divides, accompanied by efforts to build inclusive ecosystems of innovation.

Moreover, ethical foresight must become embedded in every stage of technological advancement. Developers, corporations, and governments alike bear the moral responsibility to scrutinize the consequences of the systems they seek to create. Without a clear ethical anchor guiding the democratization of technology, we risk falling into a bifurcated world of haves and have-nots, a landscape too stark to endure.

Finally, fostering collaboration between global tech superpowers—such as the United States and China—remains paramount in avoiding a collision of unchecked rivalry. Their combined influence on technology standards, innovation speed, and regulatory frameworks positions them as the ultimate arbiters of whether competition can remain constructive—or descend into chaos.

Shaping the Future with Careful Intent

The technological arms race holds transformative power, capable of redefining economies, societies, and governance alike. However, its outcomes remain uncertain, dependent on the actions nations take today to align their ambitions with the long-term good of humanity. Whether the future tilts toward increased inequality, cooperative innovation, volatile strategic shifts, or dangerous militarization lies in our collective hands, policymakers must summon the courage to adopt policies that blend prudence with ambition, closing the gap between innovation's pace and regulation's capacity. By placing ethics and foresight at the center of the race, we may not only avoid its looming dangers but also unlock its potential to uplift rather than divide, to protect rather than destroy. The stakes demand nothing less.

Recommendations for Strengthening Global Cyber Policies

As cyber threats grow and advance, countries must come together to improve global cyber rules and plans (Avance et al., 2023). To properly tackle these issues, a complete method that combines technology improvements, worldwide teamwork, and strong regulatory systems is needed (Marrone et al., 2024). Here are major suggestions focused on strengthening global cybersecurity.

Establish a Unified Global Governance Body for Cybersecurity

It is very important to create a global governance group focused on cybersecurity. This group would facilitate information sharing, create uniform security rules, and build teamwork among countries (Stavenes et al., 2020). It could also act as a central point for organizing joint cyber defense activities, enabling knowledge sharing, and encouraging best practices among its members (Eunju, 2020).

Enhance Transparency and Accountability

More openness and responsibility in cyberspace are very important for building trust and working together. Governments should be motivated to openly share information about cyber incidents and threat intelligence to improve overall awareness of situations and spot ongoing attack patterns. This kind of openness can help create a basis for better responses to upcoming dangers (Koichi A, 2019). Also, using advanced technologies can help track and ensure rules are followed, boosting the overall strength against cyber threats (Mustapha et al., 2024).

Foster Public-Private Partnerships

Working together between the tech sector and government is important for creating new cybersecurity solutions and sharing best practices (Viviano et al., 2022). Forming partnerships between public and private entities can use the knowledge and resources from both sides to improve cybersecurity preparedness and strength (Paton et al., 2010).

Integrate Cybersecurity Education and Awareness

Adding cybersecurity education and awareness programs to school and job training is important for building a strong society against cyber threats (Devanny et al., 2024). Teaching people how to identify and deal with cyber risks can greatly enhance defenses and prepare communities to respond to cyber events more effectively (Bowman et al., 2021).

Advocate for International Norms and Regulations

Promoting following international rules and regulations about cyber behavior (Erman et al., 2023). Getting countries to approve and implement agreements would aid in unifying legal standards and improving teamwork in responding to cyber incidents (Becker-Jakob et al., 2011).

Robustly Enforce Cyberattack Attribution

Using laws to strengthen the link between cyberattacks and their perpetrators can help stop bad actors and promote responsibility (ALAVI et al., 2023). When countries take strict legal action against cyber criminals, they can create a setting where cyber threats have repercussions (Kilovaty et al., 2020).

Invest in Cutting-Edge Technologies

In conclusion, investing in research and development for new technologies like quantum-resistant encryption and AI-based threat detection systems is important for keeping up with complex cyber threats (Horowitz et al., 2018). Adopting new technologies while managing their risks will be key to influencing the future of global cyber policies (Viviano et al., 2022).

Conclusion

By using these tips, countries can together reduce weaknesses, improve defenses against cyber dangers, and safeguard essential digital systems worldwide (Coulomb F et al.). With careful teamwork and forward-thinking actions, the international community can aim for a safer online environment for everyone (Coulomb F et al.). In a time when new technologies like artificial intelligence bring both chances and threats, nations need to focus on joint security actions in cyberspace (Coulomb F et al.).

References:

- Fanny Coulomb, J Paul Dunne, 2024, https://core.ac.uk/download/pdf/7170059.pdf
- Sheryn Lee, "Australian Strategic Policy Institute", 2015, https://core.ac.uk/download/pdf/30671711.pdf
- Horowitz, Michael C., "Texas National Security Review", 2018, https://core.ac.uk/download/211333744.pdf
- Erman, Eva, Furendal, Markus, Geith, Johannes, Klamberg, Mark, Lundgren, Magnus, Tallberg, Jonas, 2023, http://arxiv.org/abs/2305.11528
- Becker-Jakob, Una, "Frankfurt am Main", 2011, https://www.ssoar.info/ssoar/bitstream/document/45531/3/ssoar-2011-becker-jakob-Notions_of_Justice_in_the.pdf
- Sattar, Ihtasham, "Monterey, CA; Naval Postgraduate School", 2023, https://core.ac.uk/download/610636840.pdf
- Mustapha, Razak Abdul, "Monterey, CA; Naval Postgraduate School", 2024, https://core.ac.uk/download/618458562.pdf
- Arie Koichi, "Stockholm International Peace Research Institute", 2019, https://core.ac.uk/download/480183804.pdf
- Avance, Rosemary, Cooley, Asya, Cooley, Skye, Shin, Sumin, 2023, https://core.ac.uk/down-

load/588590640.pdf

- Alessandro Marrone, Francesco Niccolo` Moro, Maria Vittoria Massarin, Nicolo' Fasola, Sonia Lucarelli, "place:Norfolk", 2024, https://core.ac.uk/download/611898300.pdf

- Viviano, Joseph, "ScholarSpace @ JCCC", 2022, https://core.ac.uk/download/523289311.pdf

- Devanny, Joe, "FIU Digital Commons", 2024, https://core.ac.uk/download/619407279.pdf

- Bowman, Carter, "JMU Scholarly Commons", 2021, https://core.ac.uk/download/519862893.pdf

- Hagedoorn,John, Narula,Rajneesh, 2024, https://core.ac.uk/download/pdf/6937130.pdf

- Hagedoorn,John, Narula,Rajneesh, 2024, https://core.ac.uk/download/pdf/6936972.pdf

- McFarland, John W., IV, "Monterey, CA; Naval Postgraduate School", 2022, https://core.ac.uk/download/554153826.pdf

- Cimpeanu, Theodor, Han, The Anh, Lenaerts, Tom, Pereira, Lúis Moniz, Santos, Francisco C., "'Springer Science and Business Media LLC'", 2022, https://core.ac.uk/download/492530781.pdf

- Paton, Rob, Spear, Roger, "The Carnegie UK Trust", 2010, https://core.ac.uk/download/3441.pdf

- Fanny Coulomb, J Paul Dunne, 2024, https://core.ac.uk/download/pdf/7169999.pdf

- ALAVI, SEYEDHAMIDREZA, 2023, https://core.ac.uk/download/596363383.pdf
- Kilovaty, Ido, "UCI Law Scholarly Commons", 2020, https://core.ac.uk/download/328019147.pdf
- Lungu, Sorin., 2005, https://core.ac.uk/download/5076087.pdf
- Stavenes, Magnus, "'University of Agder'", 2020, https://core.ac.uk/download/351640822.pdf
- Eunju Oh, Information Security in the Cyber Era, 2020, https://core.ac.uk/download/348686559.pdf

9

ETHICAL RESPONSIBILITIES OF TECH COMPANIES IN GLOBAL AFFAIRS

Ethics in Technological Developments

As technology progresses rapidly, more controversy has arisen, especially regarding the ethics of the conduct and inventions of tech firms. It is important to critically evaluate the ethical standards and frameworks that govern technology companies, especially when they face complicated issues on a global scale. With the advent of globalization, these firms have massive resources and reach, making it all the more inevitable to look at the social impacts of their choices. The ethics of technology are central to multiple bedrock concerns, such as consumer privacy, data security, environmental concerns, diversity and inclusion, and the adoption of new technology. Such issues are germane to more than a company's operations and have far-reaching consequences on the world's economy, international relations, and the state of human rights globally.

Moreover, it is also insightful to analyze the evolution of corporate social responsibility to comprehend how ethical issues have evolved in the context of technological firms. Constructing such portraits enables us to better understand how moral and social attitudes have changed in technology and society. Every such analysis yields important lessons that can greatly benefit the current and future discourses and decisions in such contexts.

It is also important to understand the shifting nexus between the advancement of technology and core ethical problems if one is to take proactive measures to avert such issues. Technology corporations should set themselves within ethical standards based on principles of responsibility, transparency, and honesty. In embracing these values, they can be at the forefront of promoting an older and more ethically sound and ecologically sustainable international global technology environment. This paper will examine the various components of ethical problems that surround these technological advancements and the global issues these companies face and highlight the moral principles that firms require to deal with these challenges effectively.

In a world dominated by globalization, technology is evolving at an unprecedented pace. The challenges and problems caused by technology are on the rise. However, which core values should govern so that we don't lose sight of what's crucial: Ethics.

The concept of corporate social responsibility has evolved tremendously, as the engagement between firms and society has also changed dramatically. Historically, businesses were mostly concerned about maximizing profits for their shareholders while oblivious to the larger societal impact of their operations. However, with the rise of industrialization and globalization, which enhanced the influence and role of multinational corporations in world affairs, the ethical responsibilities of these companies came under intense focus.

The emergence of new regulations and labor rights movements in the 1900s coincided with the need to address harmful practices by companies. As the world moved into the mid-twentieth century, the idea that a company's responsibilities extend beyond economics was developed. Several key events, such as the publishing of Rachel Carson's famous book Silent Spring, raised awareness of the ecological consequences of business endeavors and helped bridge the gap between business activities and the welfare of society. Hence, the evolution of corporate social responsibility created an environment for the concept of ethical reasoning to be refined, including in the field of information technology.

Profit-seeking and social responsibility

Today, tech businesses face a myriad of challenges, among them the issue of how to make money without neglecting society. These businesses are key stakeholders in the economy and thus cannot afford to ignore how their operations impact society. This tension between the objectives of the investors and those of the community (Sanders et al., 2016).

While the primary objective for any business is profit-making, technology companies must understand that their decisions no longer revolve around making a profit. It is worth mentioning, to some extent, that the concept of profit maximization goes hand in hand with the concept of corporate social responsibility because profit-making should, in one way or another, serve the interest of the majority (Nizza et al., 2024). It is important to urge companies to approach a successful business in an ethical manner so that it lasts longer. They say, 'If you would picture yourself as an agency that should be making profits out of your core business only, that is a narrow business perspective.'

This immediate turnaround requires a deliberate effort to incorporate ethical perspectives across all business dimensions. In this context, ethical leadership is about the collective engagement of all relevant constituencies around the quest for common and valued goals, transparency in decision-making processes, and the building of an ethic of compliance within the organization. Furthermore, however, it should no longer be measured purely in terms of profits, as businesses must also address the impact of their creations on the environment, workers' rights and dignity, as well as the welfare of society (Nizza et al., 2024). There is a need to consider the reality of how technology transforms societal functioning and the obligation to do everything to reduce the adverse implications.

Tackling these different problems helps technology companies to establish ethical reputations and, therefore, win the trust of consumers and regulators. Key to this win-win perspective is the responsible use and management of data and technology. Tech companies should safeguard users from privacy invasion and data misuse as custodians of personal information. Moreover, they should fight against misinformation, promote digital equity, including access for all, and engage with responsible tech. By doing all this, tech firms are able to make a difference in the world through the wielding responsibility commensurate with their positions as global giants.

At the end of the day, the most important aspect for tech companies today is to strike a balance between the pursuit of profits and social responsibility. By enhancing people's welfare while trying to be profitable, these firms are earning the confidence and support of their stakeholders and becoming catalysts of great changes in the global village.

Case Studies: Ethics in Action

In this part, we examine a few case studies detailing the market and ethical impacts of global technology companies. The scope and context of these case studies provide useful understanding of contemporary ethical dilemmas, and the strategies technology companies adopt to address ethical dilemmas provide critical insights.

An interesting case demonstrates the realities of a large foreign corporation facing allegations of environmental harm and socially irresponsible behavior at its offshore factories. To address such concerns, the company has adopted a number of measures, including, but not limited to, encouraging supply chain traceability and responsible sourcing practices, thus putting ethical standards into practice as the firm extends its international reach (Burgess-Wilkerson et al. 2018).

Moreover, we will examine how a social network combats the dissemination of malicious disinformation about the network or its users, in other words, the problematic stance about freedom of expression versus content governance. In addition, when observing a foremost data analytic company, ethical concerns about protecting users' privacy and confidentiality of data become apparent, and such examination raises further questions about ethics in the context of data collection, analysis, and safeguarding (Müller et al., 2021).

These case studies underscore how ethical frameworks and decision-making processes around the globe affect the behavior and impact of tech companies. The insights gained from these examples should be useful to fresh graduates and business executives who want to mainstream ethics in forming business strategies and business models. These are truly complex ethical issues, with complex strategies to address them, which allows you to appreciate the complexities of ethical obligations in the technology industry and the importance of a social culture of ethics and responsibility within the organization.

Global Corporate Influence on the Affairs of Nations

In the 21st century, globalization has made it possible for tech companies to make decisions that target international audiences. These corporate decisions are relevant for tech diplomacy because they have the potential to grow economies, change societies, and even create or destroy international relations (Sandoval et al., 2013). Thanks to the global reach and creative power of technology companies, there is a significant influence on economies. Therefore, their decisions on issues of product development, data use, and even market interaction will affect millions of people around the globe (Burgess-Wilkerson et al., 2018).

This is especially important when the firm is addressing new markets with unique laws, customs, and cultural norms or when the firm is developing new technologies. The results of choices made within these complex environments can be far-reaching, affecting individuals and the well-being of the whole nation. Governments, non-governmental organizations, and the public more generally scrutinize the ethical dimensions of corporate behavior.

When combatting the spread of online falsehoods, fostering an inclusive digital landscape, or preserving user privacy, technology companies can no longer afford to consider the social implications of their actions solely through a local lens. At a corporate level, there is increasing focus on adopting paternalistic measures to diminish adverse outcomes as new technology evolves and not treating regulation as an adjunct to business.

At this juncture, with elevating cases of tech diplomacy, it becomes fundamental that accountability norms and standards Institutions are adhered to by multinational companies across countries. The worldwide effects of corporate decisions show the pressing need for tech companies to take a broader view that aligns with ethical governance, human rights, and sustainable development. By recognizing their role as global players, tech companies can aid in positive societal change and improve international relations. By engaging with various stakeholders and committing to transparency, tech firms can use their influence to promote meaningful progress and address major global challenges (Sandoval et al., 2013).

Regulatory Compliance and Beyond

In today's interconnected global marketplace, understanding the laws is paramount for international technology firms. Yet, for different legal regimes to be applicable, these firms also have to operate with due consideration of local economic, social, and political environments (Altenstetter et al., 1995). This signifies that such firms need to go beyond mere compliance and invest efforts in understanding different systems of rules that can help them contribute to society.

It is also crucial to work closely with national and global regulators. Technology companies must comply with and influence regulations so that they promote values that enhance society's well-being (Hall et al., 2016). This requires constructive conversations and collaborations with governments, other firms, and the public to create norms and standards that surpass ordinary legal obligations. In so doing, technology companies can even remain ahead of the curve and help set the norms and standards on emergent debates in the sector.

In addition, 'being good' entails proper law compliance and fostering a culture of ethical decision-making within the company. This culture should be present at all levels, from top management down to the last employee. Internal Controls: Promoting Risk Awareness Culture and Ethics within Organizations Transparency, accountability, and improvement should be the focus. By making it a habit, moral values will be implemented as a clear business policy that women-owned businesses should implement in social interactions with many stakeholders.

Some unethical duties include environmental degradation, abuse of human rights, and lack of diversification. All tech companies must meet the primary and secondary regulatory laws and policies. This could mean reducing the adverse effects of their products and operations on the environment, ensuring that human rights are upheld throughout their supply chains, and increasing equity and diversity within their workforce and the tech industry. These actions fall outside the core tenets of the law and reflect a greater commitment to international best practices for ethics and service to humanity.

In conclusion, obeying the law is the least that must be done. In proper ethical conduct, technology companies must aim to meet regulations and perform better by championing ethics, interacting with stakeholders, and implementing the full scope of corporate social responsibilities while penetrating international markets. So doing means that they will commit themselves to the morality of their practice and improve the world's welfare.

Participation and Openness to Stakeholders

Technology companies in international relations have responsibilities that extend beyond rules. It begins with stakeholder engagement and a willingness to be open. Technology addresses a variety of issues that affect stakeholders, including constituents such as governments, customers, employees, and the broader community. Therefore, technology companies are encouraged to engage and collaborate with these groups (Now A, 2018).

This engagement implies the need to be attentive to what stakeholders say and consider the information provided in decision-making. Technology companies are able to earn confidence and establish relations with stakeholders by ensuring there is communication. Transparency is very important for this engagement. Companies should seek to provide adequate and easily understood and explained information on their products and services, functions, and daily activities. It has become a necessity for the stakeholders to understand the risks associated with data usage and the social impact that the technologies are targeting to build their confidence (Nolan C et al., 2008).

By dividing their responsibilities towards the stakeholders, companies can enhance their reputation management. The stakeholders are able to measure their ethical behavior by being well-informed about the company's business activities, environmental impacts, and social involvements. Transparency implies seeking issues from the stakeholders and answering them when needed. Ordinary conversations, polls, and forums show the intention to hear and act. This way of doing things can help make better ethical decisions and disclose potential pitfalls.

Furthermore, media and academia made it very clear that technology companies that want to comply with openness and accountability must come out about their problems and failures. By offering one's shortcomings and intent to overcome them, companies may exhibit lowliness and genuine commitment towards rectifying ethics. Ultimately, the consumption of stakeholders and information and communication technologies are integral parts of responsibility as a global citizen for technology companies. It is believed that revealing their stakeholders to their activities and being more transparent about the activities and the impacts created would offer an opportunity for technology companies to take part in building a more ethical and sustainable global technology system.

Business Ethics in the Emerging Economies

There has been an escalating concern with the ethical challenges of technology companies in the context of developing economies as technology further permeates global business operations (Sandoval et al., 2013). These markets are growing rapidly and have more advanced forms of technology and divergent cultures and regulatory regimes, thereby creating particular ethical dimensions that need attention. An important consideration in this debate is the tension between the eagerness to grow the business and the need to be ethical. In technological progression, such companies are most likely to encounter situations where local customs, laws, and practices are not in unison with the general international ethical code. This scenario underscores the need for a more nuanced understanding of where the business outcomes are achieved within acceptable ethical boundaries(Chater et al. 2007).

Moreover, emerging markets and the middle class are constantly being economically distorted due to the seemingly ever-increasing injection of Western technology, which begs the question: is this ethical? The gush of disruptive technologies can potentially cause dramatic revolutions in society's social fabric and economy. Hence, tech companies must consider their products' implications for people living in more information- and resource-devoid regions(Sandoval et al., 2013).

One key aspect of recognizing and addressing ethical issues is engaging with local stakeholders and context, as many facets are involved. Such a policy calls for an investment in mutual trust and respect. To a varying degree, responsible technology and ethics-compliant innovation in emerging markets are also determined by responsible practices. Such initiatives may, for example, include funding programs for education and training in digital skills, helping local communities, and supporting governments and NGOs to ensure that technology is used in an ethical way.

Taking such steps further, technology companies will create favorable conditions for developing their firms and countries technologically advanced and ethically clean developing countries.

Engaging a Technological Organization for a Fairer Country

There is a need to constantly generate an ethical perspective on the innovation process by engaging the entire organization at all levels to make a change (Lengnick-Hall et al., 2003). This culture goes beyond just following laws and making money, showing the importance of how technology affects people and communities worldwide (Elder et al.).

In order for this goal to be realized, tech organizations need to bring ethical consideration in all the major processes, thereby fostering a strong desire to be ethical in all activities. This combined might also entail the use of ethics training in induction courses for new employees, the formulation of strict ethical guidelines regarding producing goods, and the protection of teams that raise ethical issues from retribution (Charter et al., 2007).

Moreover, tech leaders have a huge responsibility to foster and model ethical behavior and, in doing so, the organizational culture. It is important to emphasize that for innovation ethics to be effective, informant accountability must be established. This task encompasses nurturing a culture of freely speaking about ethical dilemmas and enabling multi-stakeholder participation in assessing the ethical implications of tech projects (Elder et al.).

Cultivating an environment with a strong ethical work culture, interplay of ideas and knowledge within the workplace enables tech companies to mitigate some of the issues that come with innovation. In addition, engaging with other actors, such as community groups, universities, or regulatory bodies, may enrich the ethical principles that provide a framework for the conduct of tech firms (Charter et al., 2007).

Collaboration with these associations helps gain valuable experience, identifies potential ethical dilemmas, and assists in formulating universal ethical principles in different domains. Taking such an ethical innovation perspective, the firms in this sector not only conform to society's expectations but also enhance their credibility, thus consolidating their position as responsible global actors (Elder et al.).

In the end, building a culture of ethical innovation requires ongoing efforts to weave ethical ideas into the company's structure, understanding that ethical behavior and technological progress are closely connected goals for the future.

Future Directions for Responsible Tech

As technology changes, the future brings both exciting opportunities and serious difficulties for responsible tech practices. Tech companies must take a forward-looking stance, prioritizing ethical concerns at every step of innovation and use.

A major part of responsible tech in the future is applying ethical principles of Artificial Intelligence to creating AI systems. This requires a promise to be open, fair, and accountable and to carry out detailed societal impact reviews during the AI design stages while also tackling possible biases and ethical issues (Orts et al., 2001).

Also, new technologies like quantum computing and biotechnology require proactive discussions and rules to ensure ethical use while reducing risks (Altenstetter et al., 1995). Teaming up with industry leaders, policymakers, and ethicists will be important for establishing strong governance that addresses the complex aspects of these emerging technologies.

In addition, since technology development is global, joint efforts are needed to create international standards for responsible tech practices. Encouraging cooperation across borders and open discussions will help align ethical guidelines and regulations, leading to a united approach to ethical innovation worldwide (Altenstetter et al., 1995).

Another key area for future responsible tech is improving corporate social responsibility within tech firms. This means not only charitable efforts but also building a strong culture of ethics, caring for the environment, and understanding societal effects at all company levels. Additionally, allowing employees to voice ethical issues and creating ways to engage in ethical decision-making will be important for building a responsible culture in tech firms.

Lastly, the path to responsible tech requires continuous education and awareness programs to boost digital literacy, ethical thinking, and critical reasoning skills among today's and tomorrow's technology users. Teaching individuals the knowledge and skills to make informed ethical choices in their tech interactions will help society create a more sustainable and responsible tech environment.

In summary, navigating the future of responsible tech needs a complete approach that includes multiple parties, recognizing the changing nature of technology advancements and the ongoing ethical challenges they bring. By adopting this mindset, tech companies can promote sustainable and ethical innovations while laying the groundwork for a tech-driven future focused on ethics and societal welfare.

References:

- Sandoval, M., "'Informa UK Limited'", 2013, https://core.ac.uk/download/18295062.pdf

- Charter, Martin, Clark, Tom, 2007, https://core.ac.uk/download/103312.pdf

- Burgess-Wilkerson, Barbara, Garrison, Chlotia, Hamilton, Clovia, Robbins, Keith, 2018, https://core.ac.uk/download/214444219.pdf

- Altenstetter, Christa., 1995, https://core.ac.uk/download/5079662.pdf

- Hall, Kath, Regan, Milton C., Jr., "FLASH: The Fordham Law Archive of Scholarship and History", 2016, https://core.ac.uk/download/144231468.pdf

- Access Now, 2018, https://core.ac.uk/download/233087372.pdf

- Chris Nolan, Racheal Yeager, "BSR", 2008, https://core.ac.uk/download/71352339.pdf

- Elder, Jakob, Kuhlmann, Stefan, Smits, Ruud, 2024, https://core.ac.uk/download/pdf/6428270.pdf

- Sanders, Samuel, "SURFACE at Syracuse University", 2016, https://core.ac.uk/download/215706921.pdf

- Nizza, Virginia Consuelo, 2024, https://core.ac.uk/download/612336188.pdf

- Dine, J, Koutsias, M, "'Edward Elgar Publishing'", 2013, https://core.ac.uk/download/16388018.pdf

- Orts, Eric W., 2001, https://core.ac.uk/download/524862765.pdf

- Müller, Vincent C., 2021, https://core.ac.uk/download/305120702.pdf

10

Establishing Global Regulatory Frameworks for Emerging Technologies

Regulatory Challenges

ORIGINALLY REGARDED AS AN impediment, the legal environment of new technologies is today seen as a major factor determining how governments, large corporations, and global institutions conduct their affairs. As technology development spins, former regulations cannot move fast enough to keep pace with artificial intelligence, biotechnology, and quantum computing developments. One fundamental problem is the lack of commonality among the said technologies, and each has its own ethical, security, and societal issues that will require distinct regulatory regimes. Moreover, since these technologies are usually international in scope, universal standards become hard to develop since events in one state have repercussions in other countries, which have different sets of problems. To compound the problem further, the internationalization of cyberspace now makes it even harder to regulate technology that is beyond traditional nation-states. The fast rate at which technology evolves puts forth further challenges, as ever-changing risks mean that regulation must be made to stimulate innovation.

Also, the ambiguity regarding new technologies makes it difficult for regulators to forecast the eventual consequences when coping with changing technological capabilities. The interactions between government agencies, the private sector, the providers of political and social services, and scholars also make it more difficult to address fully the problem of setting up regulatory structures calling for joint responsibility on a number of diverse issues of technology governance. Furthermore, the existence of different national priorities, various policy and institutional preferences, and differing cultural values also add a different layer of challenge in formulating new and emerging technologies regulation at the global level. In this light, working through different opinions and dealing with political conflicts is crucial when creating and implementing appropriate policies. This section examines the global aspects of regulating emergent practices, emphasizing the need for a global view to address technology evolution's diverse and complex nature.

General Background to Regulation of Technology

Technology systems management has been a significant activity in the world's political arena since the onset of industrialization. There have always been disagreements between rules that allow the use of technology and the urgent necessity to protect society from its possible and latent menace. Numerous legislations for the control of the use of technology for safe and ethical purposes in industries such as transport, telecommunications, and energy, among others, were instituted, especially in the first half of the 20th century. These rules helped shape the future of technology governance and define frameworks for countries to work together on regulation issues. The proliferation of digital technologies from the late twentieth century and into the twenty-first made matters more challenging for regulators. The characteristically free nature of cyberspace, coupled with the internationalization of digital platforms, overshot the boundaries of existing regulatory frameworks, thereby seeking out new approaches to governance. Data protection, cybersecurity, patents, and globalization were born as important issues that called for regulatory action, thus reinstating legal regimes and international treaties (Feng et al., 2008).

Apart from those, such past events as the increase in nuclear technologies and the arms race to the control of hardware also stressed the need for effective regulatory measures to manage such risky technologies. The establishment of international organizations demonstrated the necessity of collaboration for solving common problems and risks associated with the development of technology. The course of regulation of technology, on the other hand, also tells of the evolution of the perception of the impact of these developments on civilization. As technologies became more prevalent in the day to day activities, society started to focus on the implications of their use. More notably, the discussion of genetic modification issues and the responsibilities attached to artificial intelligence shifted more toward ethical and social concerns. Such a historical perspective on the evolution of technology regulations is an interesting story from which today's policymakers can learn and gain useful lessons. It is crucial to comprehend both what has worked in the past in establishing regulatory frameworks and what has not in order to inform the development of modern, efficient, and adaptive regulatory regimes for new technologies. By understanding past lessons, different actors can achieve a good balance between technological advancement and its governance that preserves a conducive atmosphere for technology development and mechanisms for the world's well-being.

International Regulatory Organizations and Their Significance

In order to cope with advanced technologies at a global level, it is necessary to comprehend the functions of international regulatory organizations. These intermediaries are crucial in establishing regulations, facilitating states' relations, and dealing with globalization issues. The global aspect of technology and its effects calls for an integrated and coordinated approach to regulation (Communications A and Authority M). Among the most visible international organizations of the regulatory kind, the International Telecommunication Union, the World Trade Organization, and the International Organization for Standardization play a vital role in developing and applying policies and regulations for new technologies. For example, the International Telecommunication Union helps to ensure that global telecommunication policies advance cross-border interconnected systems and mutual equity of citizens of the state over cross-border communication.

Also, the World Trade Organization has a good influence in managing the trade dimensions that arise from technological regulation, aiming to decrease the impediments to global commerce caused by different rules and standards. The World Trade Organization also helps to harmonize technology products and services trade regulation worldwide by promoting transparency and fair practices (Hoekman et al., 2017). Schmidt and colleagues emphasize the importance of the International Organization for Standardization in conjunction with these organizations as a signatory and founding member in formulating internationally accepted technical standards. Such standards apply to a wide range of sectors, including IT, cybersecurity, and environment, serving as basic requirements meant to guarantee universality and standardization. Regional authorities, such as the European Union Agency for Cybersecurity and the Asia-Pacific Telecommunity, also shape the regulatory landscape for adopting new technologies in their regions. These organizations foster cooperation, information sharing, and capability building, which helps to harmonize regulatory frameworks at the regional and international levels. While the scope of international regulatory bodies is to set standards and define guidelines, their role extends to the monitoring and compliance of the set standards, advocating for proper utilization practices, and facilitating discussions and sharing of experiences among various stakeholders.

Organizations today need to be adaptable if they are to survive global competition. They need to continuously revise their frameworks as changes occur, guarding against the dangers while positioning themselves to exploit the opportunities that the development of new technologies and integration into the world society entails.

Examples: Global Integration and Regulation of Technology

Understanding how a major international regulation was created for adjusting genetically modified seeds into farming requires a deeper examination of the good practice models – in this case study, genetic erosion. For example, The Codex Alimentarius Commission has established an international trade model for genetically modified organisms that will eradicate world poverty through trade. This kind of collaboration speaks to how multinational organizations are able to deal with regulatory concerns that are difficult to deal with in silos (Ona-Olapo A et al., 2024). Another important case is the Montreal Protocol, a good example of global management on environmental issues. This treaty has successfully banned the manufacture and consumption of ozone-depleting chemicals and is a clear indicator of how urgent technological challenges can be dealt with through multilateral agreements (Kazimi J et al., 2024).

Additionally, how the International Telecommunication Union manages the radio frequency spectrum also provides a perspective on how regulatory frameworks can facilitate the rapid advancement and harmonized deployment of wireless technologies worldwide. These examples, therefore, also underline the necessity for international work and the practice of consensus-building in the context of developing appropriate and powerful policies on new technologies. These successful experiences should also be useful to policymakers and other stakeholders to determine the principles and practices of effective global governance for technological advancement.

Regulation Follows Policy Innovation

Such approaches are vital for any technology in a world of constant technological evolution. Automation to Work regulation is equally vital to business leaders, stakeholders, and the world. This equilibrium is essential in determining how the use of technology would progress and where the adverse effects can be avoided or controlled. The encouragement of innovation is essential since it enhances economic growth, jobs, and social welfare.

Throughout human history, innovation has sparked revolutionary changes that have reshaped our world. Stop. Think about the smartphone in your pocket – a device that would seem like magic to someone from just 50 years ago. The imperative to foster innovation burns bright, yet it dances a complex waltz with regulatory frameworks that must evolve quickly (Falkner et al., 2012). Like a double-helix structure, innovation and regulation intertwine, each supporting and constraining the other in an endless spiral toward progress.

Consider this: while technological breakthroughs surge forward like a rushing river, regulation follows – sometimes stumbling, sometimes sprinting – to channel these waters safely. Privacy concerns explode. Security threats multiply. Ethical dilemmas emerge from the shadows. These challenges demand sophisticated regulatory responses that can protect without suffocating innovation (Aboy et al., 2023). Trust, that fragile bridge between public acceptance and technological advancement, must be carefully constructed and vigilantly maintained.

How do we strike the right balance? Smart regulation isn't a one-size-fits-all straightjacket. Instead, picture a risk-based approach that adapts and flexes like a living organism. Some innovations need tight controls; others thrive with lighter-touch oversight. The key? Identifying potential hazards early, when course corrections are still possible, and before unintended consequences can cascade into disasters.

Collaboration isn't just important – it's absolutely vital. Picture a round table where government officials, tech entrepreneurs, academic researchers, and community advocates gather to forge solutions. These diverse voices, each bringing unique insights and concerns, create a symphony of perspectives that enriches regulatory frameworks. Sometimes they clash. Often they harmonize. Always, they contribute to a more nuanced understanding of how to promote responsible innovation.

The regulatory landscape must be both rigid and fluid – an apparent contradiction that makes perfect sense in practice. Clear boundaries provide certainty, while principle-based approaches offer the flexibility to handle tomorrow's challenges. It's like building a house with both concrete foundations and moveable walls, ready to adapt as needs change.

The path forward demands an unwavering commitment to evidence-based decision-making. We must measure impacts, analyze outcomes, and adjust course when needed. Global cooperation becomes not just desirable but essential, as technology knows no borders. Through this complex dance of innovation and regulation, we can harness technology's transformative power while keeping its potential dangers in check.

Stakeholder Engagement and Consensus Building

In the quest for effective global technology regulation, stakeholder engagement emerges as both a cornerstone and catalyst - a complex dance of diverse perspectives seeking harmonious resolution. Within this intricate tapestry, governments, corporations, scholarly minds, civil society champions, and everyday citizens must interweave their distinct viewpoints to forge meaningful regulatory frameworks (Chaturvedi et al., 2015). Like a masterful orchestra, each stakeholder contributes unique notes to this regulatory symphony, creating rich harmonies that echo through society's corridors, economics' marketplace, and ethics' sacred halls.

Yet beneath this idealistic surface lurks a thorny reality: stakeholders, armed with conflicting agendas and specialized knowledge domains, often clash in a cacophony of competing interests. Some voices boom while others whisper. Technical expertise collides with practical wisdom. Corporate imperatives challenge public good.

The art lies in cultivating an ecosystem where every voice resonates. Through crystalline communication channels, collaborative problem-solving laboratories, and the delicate alignment of disparate goals, pathways to consensus gradually materialize - like morning fog lifting to reveal common ground (Falkner et al., 2012). This transformative process demands patience, but its rewards ripple beyond any regulatory framework.

A crucial step in consensus-building is recognizing and accommodating different groups' diverse interests and values. For instance, technology developers often prioritize innovation and growth, while policymakers and civil society may focus on risk mitigation and societal benefits. Robust stakeholder engagement initiatives require proactive regulatory leadership that fosters open dialogues, promotes iterative feedback, and ensures that dissenting voices are reflected in the final regulatory frameworks. Transparency and accountability are equally vital ingredients in this process, fostering trust, ensuring equitable representation, and ultimately producing regulatory models rooted in cooperation.

Beyond technical outcomes, meaningful stakeholder engagement must focus on ethical considerations and human rights. As emerging technologies increasingly influence privacy, security, and access, regulatory discussions must prioritize frameworks that preserve core societal values, including inclusivity and fairness (Chaturvedi et al., 2015). By fostering dialogue on these critical topics, regulatory authorities can align policy decisions with broader social priorities. Ultimately, enabling productive engagement and consensus among diverse stakeholders enhances the legitimacy and robustness of global regulatory approaches, ensuring a balanced governance model that supports both technological innovation and societal well-being.

Impact of Regulation on Technology Development

The intersection of regulation and technological development is a defining feature of the modern innovation landscape. Carefully designed regulatory frameworks can powerfully influence the trajectory of emerging technologies, fostering a balance between rapid advancement and responsible governance. Effective regulations can catalyze innovation by providing clear benchmarks and encouraging industries to achieve compliance while navigating development with confidence. On the other hand, a heavy-handed or fragmented regulatory approach risks stifling innovation and creating uneven global progress (Huzair et al., 2011).

Well-crafted regulatory measures establish stable environments conducive to investment, offering innovators clear expectations and reducing the uncertainty associated with high-speed technological evolution (Falkner et al., 2012). For instance, in emerging sectors such as artificial intelligence and biotechnology, rules that emphasize transparency, ethical accountability, and risk management safeguard societal interests and steer innovation towards more sustainable and inclusive outcomes. This regulatory foresight encourages businesses to allocate resources for research and development that align with long-term societal goals.

Nevertheless, overly complex or restrictive regulations can exert a chilling effect. Excessive legal demands, unclear standards, or unaligned international protocols can create red tape that deters startups and emerging players from entering markets. These risks underscore the importance of developing flexible, context-aware regulatory frameworks that evolve alongside technological advancements. For example, sectors like blockchain technology or quantum computing demand agile guidelines that address risks while supporting experimentation and scaling.

Regulations also impact global competitiveness by shaping the accessibility of certain markets. Countries with harmonized rules are better positioned to facilitate cross-border innovation and trade, while regulatory disparities may lead to fragmented markets or diminished global adoption. Striking a balance between predictability, adaptability, and inclusivity is thus fundamental. By actively addressing emerging challenges and incorporating long-term societal values, regulation can act not as a barrier but as a stepping-stone to sustainable technological progress.

The Role of Public-Private Partnerships in Regulation

Public-private partnerships (PPPs) are emerging as a cornerstone of effective global technology regulation. These collaborative frameworks between governments and industry players address modern technologies' inherent complexity and dynamism, which often exceed the capacity of traditional regulatory systems (Egenhofer et al., 2008). Leveraging complementary expertise from public and private entities ensures that regulatory initiatives are technically sound but also practical and forward-looking.

Private-sector involvement brings critical technical and industry-specific knowledge to regulatory discussions, offering invaluable insights into emerging trends, operational feasibility, and market needs. This enables governments to craft policies that balance innovation with safety and accountability. For example, in the regulation of artificial intelligence, private-sector input ensures that policymakers understand the technical nuances of algorithmic design, bias mitigation, and transparency. Similarly, in renewable energy technologies, PPPs facilitate collaboration on sustainability standards, enabling scalable and cost-effective adoption across regions (Hall et al.).

At the same time, governments in PPPs provide the ethical and public welfare oversight necessary to safeguard societal interests. Facilitating these partnerships builds trust and legitimacy, as private-sector voices are integrated into decision-making, fostering a culture of shared responsibility. Trust is further enhanced through transparency and knowledge-sharing mechanisms—key elements of successful PPPs—that ensure a continuous flow of information between stakeholders. Collaborative frameworks also pave the way for developing unified, internationally recognized standards that transcend regional regulatory disparities while addressing global challenges like cybersecurity and sustainability.

Strong governance protocols are essential to prevent potential pitfalls—such as regulatory capture, where private interests undermine public welfare. These protocols include ensuring transparency, defining ethical codes of conduct, and instituting accountability safeguards to maintain a fair balance between profit-driven motives and the broader public good. In view of these dynamics, effective and ethically anchored public-private partnerships stand at the forefront of modern regulation, enabling governments and industry to co-create regulatory solutions that uphold fairness while unlocking technological potential.

Future Trends in Technology Regulation

The dizzying pace of technological change presents unprecedented regulatory challenges, necessitating future-proofed approaches to governance. One prominent future trend involves the intensification of data privacy regulations in response to mounting concerns about breaches and misuse. As digital interconnectedness grows, regulations that prioritize cross-border data protections and impose stricter requirements on handling personal information will likely dominate the global agenda (Falkner et al., 2012). Emerging technologies such as AI and machine learning will also require tailored rules addressing ethical dimensions, including fairness, transparency, and accountability in algorithm design and deployment.

The rise of powerful technologies, including quantum computing and biotechnology, will present more complex dilemmas. Regulatory frameworks tailored to assessing risks and ethical challenges stemming from these fields must emerge. Quantum computing, for example, will necessitate standards that address its potential to disrupt cybersecurity protocols, whereas biotechnology will require comprehensive regulations mitigating risks to health, biodiversity, and social equality (Berry et al., 2015). As regulators grapple with such complexities, they will need greater collaboration with tech leaders and ethicists to ensure governance strategies remain both innovative and inclusive.

Additionally, sustainability is poised to become a critical lens through which regulations are formulated. As climate change pressures intensify, directives promoting eco-conscious technology development, resource efficiency, and lifecycle sustainability will take precedence. Regulatory trends may increasingly emphasize circular economy frameworks, mandating standards around resource recovery, eco-friendly designs, and waste minimization. Such measures could be accompanied by international initiatives harmonizing sustainability-related technology standards across borders.

Moreover, integrating technology into nearly every domain of society will accelerate the need for cybersecurity-focused regulations. As increasingly vital infrastructure relies on digital ecosystems, enhanced cyber-resilience standards, incident response frameworks, and global data-sharing agreements will become integral regulatory components. The trend towards "regulatory sandboxes"—experimental settings enabling real-time testing of new technologies within controlled conditions—may also gain traction, offering innovators a responsive yet risk-averse space to develop solutions.

In summary, the future of technology regulation will hinge on balancing tailored, flexible policies with robust ethical safeguards and global cooperation. By addressing emerging risks while promoting equitable and sustainable development, the frameworks of tomorrow will help shape a more inclusive, resilient, and innovation-driven society.

Conclusion: Pathways to Effective Global Governance

In the intricate labyrinth of emerging technologies, the imperative for sophisticated global governance mechanisms has crystallized with unprecedented urgency. The trajectory of technological regulation hinges precariously on our collective capacity to orchestrate nimble, adaptive responses to the kaleidoscopic transformations occurring across multifarious domains. Effective global governance necessitates an intricate choreography between nation-states, transnational entities, and commercial enterprises.

The cornerstone of exemplary governance lies in orchestrating harmonized regulatory frameworks that address the far-reaching reverberations of technological innovation. This synchronization catalyzes meaningful dialogue among diverse stakeholders, fostering ecosystems that nurture breakthrough innovations while establishing robust safeguards against potential hazards. The strategic alignment of regulatory paradigms across jurisdictions diminishes fragmentation and accelerates cross-border collaboration.

A comprehensive approach to global governance mandates equitable representation across the stakeholder spectrum (Chaturvedi et al., 2015). Integrating perspectives from developing nations, marginalized communities, and civil society organizations proves indispensable in crafting regulations that comprehensively address the multifaceted implications of technological advancement. Through this inclusive framework, global governance mechanisms can champion equity, answerability, and lucidity principles.

Cultivating interdisciplinary synergies emerges as another critical determinant of effective governance (Chaturvedi et al., 2015). Given the labyrinthine nature of technological progress, the convergence of policy architects, technical virtuosos, ethical philosophers, and legal luminaries becomes paramount. This multidisciplinary fusion enriches the understanding of technological ramifications and facilitates the development of balanced regulatory architectures.

Implementing adaptive regulatory frameworks is crucial in navigating the tempestuous waters of technological evolution (Chaturvedi et al., 2015). Such flexibility enables governance systems to respond dynamically to the meteoric advancement of artificial intelligence, biotechnology, and quantum computing. Continuous assessment and iterative refinement prove vital in ensuring the sustained efficacy of global technology governance. Regular scrutiny of existing regulatory mechanisms, coupled with the integration of cutting-edge scientific insights and societal feedback, maintains their relevance amid technological flux (Chaturvedi et al., 2015).

In synthesis, the quest for exemplary global governance in nascent technologies demands a multifaceted strategy encompassing harmonization, inclusivity, interdisciplinary collaboration, adaptability, and perpetual evolution. Through adherence to these principles, the international community can forge responsible, progressive regulatory frameworks that simultaneously catalyze innovation and safeguard ethical considerations, security imperatives, and equitable outcomes.

References:

- Falkner, Robert, Jaspers, Nico, "'MIT Press - Journals'", 2012, https://core.ac.uk/download/223650.pdf

- Aboy, Mateo, Brongersma, Mark, Cohen, I. Glenn, De Jong, Eline, Floridi, Luciano, Gasser, Urs, Kop, Mauritz, Laflamme, Raymond, Minssen, Timo, Quintel, Teresa, 2023, http://arxiv.org/abs/2303.16671

- Adeola Ona-Olapo, Esho, Tosin Daniel Iluyomade, Tosin Michael Olatunde, Osayi Philip Igbinenikaro, "International Journal of Engineering Research Updates", 2024, https://www.semanticscholar.org/paper/33ad768042e8151b56d4e2c46d14cc3f4c84aa2e

- Jamshid Kazimi, Harshita Thalwal, "2024 7th International Conference on Green Technology and Sustainable Development (GTSD)", 2024, https://www.semanticscholar.org/paper/64e35122c519fc2f0404921af98648231c2011a7

- Berry, Pam M., Brown, Iain, Everard, Mark, Firbank, Les G., Harrison, Paula A., Lundy, Lian, Quine, Chris P., Rowan, John S., Wade, Rebecca, Watts, Kevin, 2015, https://core.ac.uk/download/141567357.pdf

- Chaturvedi, Sachin, Ladikas, Miltos, Stemerding, Dirk, Zhao, Yandong, "'Springer Science and Business Media LLC'", 2015, https://core.ac.uk/download/42136809.pdf

- Huzair, Farah, Kale, Dinar, "Innogen",

2011, https://core.ac.uk/download/109590.pdf

- Australian Communications and Media Authority, "Australian Communications and Media Authority", 2024, https://core.ac.uk/download/pdf/30671507.pdf

- Hoekman, Bernard, Schuman, Robert, 2017, https://core.ac.uk/download/322823606.pdf

- Feng, L., Moodley, K., "Arcom", 2008,

- Hall, Andy, Kingiri, Ann, 2024, https://core.ac.uk/download/pdf/6480582.pdf

- Egenhofer, Christian., Fujiwara, Noriko, 2008, https://core.ac.uk/download/5082065.pdf

- Kariuki Nyaga, Joseph, 2024, https://core.ac.uk/download/pdf/6618321.pdf

11

TECHNOLOGICAL SOVEREIGNTY AND NATIONAL SECURITY

Technological Sovereignty: A Multidimensional Imperative

IN AN EPOCH INCREASINGLY defined by relentless technological advancement and its pervasive influence, technological sovereignty has crystallized into a pivotal element for nations asserting authority over their digital and technological landscapes. Beyond mere infrastructure management, this concept serves as an expansive framework essential for securing economic stability, augmenting geopolitical influence, and—most critically—fortifying national security. As revolutionary breakthroughs continue to reshape global paradigms, the intricate balance between self-reliance and the tapestry of global interconnectedness emerges as a fundamental challenge for nations maneuvering to preserve their sovereignty in a swiftly evolving digital ecosystem.

Historically, the landscape of national security has experienced seismic shifts; it has transitioned from the tangible defenses of physical borders to the abstract yet critical realm of cyber defense and digital resilience. Contemporary security narratives now intricately weave traditional military imperatives with emerging threats—cyberattacks, digital espionage, and the fraught dependencies of global supply chains. The infusion of technology into these security strategies has amplified the complexities surrounding sovereignty, unveiling vulnerabilities that would have been inconceivable in prior epochs. This labyrinthine array of technological dependence underscores the pressing need for nations to reevaluate the frameworks through which they exercise control over their technological assets.

The Conundrum of Technological Autonomy in a Globalized World

In the 21st century, technological sovereignty necessitates a dual capacity that allows nations to remain autonomous while engaging constructively in the global ecosystem. The interconnected nature of modern economies and intricate digital systems revolutionizes national infrastructures, simultaneously rendering them increasingly vulnerable to external adversities. Cyberattacks targeting critical infrastructure—electric grids, financial systems, and defense installations—are stark reminders of the existential threats nations contend with when their cyber ecosystems become susceptible to exploitation. Moreover, foreign actors' breaches in sensitive technologies and intellectual property heighten the stakes of maintaining proprietary control in an intensely globalized industrial landscape.

Yet, paradoxically, global supply chains thrive as the lifeblood of technological innovation, enabling the swift advancement of cutting-edge systems and cross-border collaborations. However, therein lies the paradox: while these networks enhance efficiency and foster innovation, they simultaneously propagate dependencies, binding many nations to foreign entities for vital components. This reliance introduces vulnerabilities; disruptions—from geopolitical conflicts, coercive policies, or abrupt supply chain bottlenecks—can directly undermine national security objectives. This precarious equilibrium between interdependence and autonomy underscores the broader dilemma policymakers face as they strive to achieve technological self-sufficiency without isolating themselves from the myriad benefits of globalization.

Securing Sovereignty through Strategic Investments and Policy Interventions

To navigate this convoluted landscape adeptly, governments must embrace multifaceted strategies that simultaneously reinforce domestic capabilities and mitigate external risks. Central to this initiative is prioritizing investments in research and development (R&D). By nurturing indigenous technological expertise, nations can diminish their dependence on foreign sources, thereby enhancing economic resilience and strategic autonomy. Furthermore, diversifying supply chains becomes a crucial countermeasure, curtailing the risks associated with overreliance on a singular region or supplier.

Equally paramount is the establishment of robust cybersecurity frameworks. Fortifying digital infrastructure against cyber incursions, espionage, and data breaches is essential in safeguarding national sovereignty. Public-private partnerships have emerged as crucial mechanisms, harnessing the innovative prowess of private entities while symbiotically aligning them with national security imperatives. Additionally, fostering international cooperation on technology governance, cybersecurity norms, and trade regulations becomes vital in addressing vulnerabilities that transcend geographical boundaries. While technological sovereignty inherently champions autonomy, the interconnected fabric of global threats necessitates collaborative responses to challenges, including cybercrime, intellectual property theft, and the insidious misuse of technology.

The Historical Arc of National Security and the Technological Dimension

National security has perpetually been a fluid construct molded by the ever-evolving socioeconomic, geopolitical, and technological pressures of the era. Early civilizations concentrated on fortifying territorial borders, yet as time unfolded, the conception of security expanded to encompass economic stability, societal cohesion, and strategic resilience. The transformative impacts of the Industrial Revolution—and later the Digital Revolution—profoundly redefined security parameters, rendering technology not merely a tool but also a contested domain of competition, conflict, and influence.

The Cold War era epitomized the escalating significance of technology within security paradigms, showcasing advancements in nuclear armaments and space exploration as symbols of national might. In contemporary times, the digital revolution has catalyzed a comparable shift, albeit with an emphasis on information technologies, artificial intelligence, quantum computing, and biotechnology. Such innovations, while heralding unmatched opportunities, have also introduced an array of vulnerabilities. Modern threats have transcended the physical battlegrounds; they thrive in the shadows of cyberspace, manipulating technologies to undermine sovereignty, destabilize economies, and erode societal trust.

Recently, nontraditional risks—including pandemics, climate crises, and social unrest—have converged with technological dimensions in unpredictable ways, further complicating national security strategies. These interwoven risks highlight the imperative for adaptive and forward-thinking security frameworks capable of addressing both overt external threats and subtle systemic vulnerabilities.

Technology and Sovereignty: Interdependence and Competition

In the current global milieu, technological sovereignty intertwines intricately with geopolitical influence. Nations that command cutting-edge technologies stand in a dominant position to assert authority, expand their influence, and secure economic leadership. For instance, prowess in artificial intelligence, quantum computing, and 5G telecommunications has become integral not only to economic competitiveness but also to defense capabilities and global strategic standing.

Yet, the unrelenting pace of technological progress births a perennial tension between innovation and vulnerability. The integration of global supply chains, data systems, and technological infrastructures has engendered unprecedented interdependencies, magnifying the risks of economic coercion and foreign manipulation. These dependencies challenge the very essence of traditional sovereignty, particularly in instances where critical technologies lie under external control or experience disruptions from multinational corporations or foreign governments.

Simultaneously, nations lacking sufficient technological capacity risk descending into subordinate roles within the global hierarchy, effectively ceding portions of their sovereignty to more advanced countries. This dynamic underscores the competitive dimensions of technology, where the pursuit of leadership intertwines with the safeguarding of national interests and the shaping of international engagement rules.

Charting the Future: Sovereignty in a Digital Age

The interplay between technology and sovereignty mandates a continuous reassessment of national policies, international collaborations, and innovation strategies. As emerging technologies increasingly sculpt global power structures, maintaining sovereignty necessitates not merely strengthening domestic capabilities but also engaging the international community to forge equitable frameworks for technological governance. The delicate balance between autonomy and global interconnectedness will inherently define the contours of national sovereignty in the ensuing decades; nations that effectively navigate this complexity are poised to emerge as leaders on the world stage.

Ultimately, the quest for technological sovereignty must harmonize the promotion of innovation with the mitigation of inherent risks, forging a pathway empowering states to protect their independence while embracing the collaborative ethos of globalization. In this pursuit, countries can uphold the ideals of sovereignty while adeptly adapting to the imperatives of an interconnected and perpetually evolving technological landscape. The endeavor for technological autonomy will undoubtedly remain a decisive factor in ensuring national security, bolstering economic resilience, and navigating a world where technology transcends mere utility to become a profound domain of power and influence.

Case Studies on Technological Autonomy

In the relentless quest for technological autonomy, a plethora of case studies illustrates the intricate complexities and multifaceted nuances inherent in achieving digital sovereignty. One striking exemplar emerges from China's deliberate strategies aimed at amplifying its domestic tech industry. This ambition manifests vividly in its comprehensive plan to elevate the nation to a commanding position in advanced manufacturing and innovation, thus aspiring to minimize reliance on foreign technologies and ensure self-sufficiency across critical sectors (Cottey et al., 2022). This concerted effort epitomizes not only the strategic allocation of resources but also robust governmental support and targeted industrial policies crafted to augment the nation's technological self-sufficiency.

In stark contrast, the European Union's implementation of the General Data Protection Regulation (GDPR) serves as an illuminating case study in promoting digital sovereignty through regulatory frameworks (Gunnarsson J). By instituting stringent data protection protocols and championing individual privacy rights, the EU seeks to assert greater dominion over personal data while diminishing dependencies on foreign technological infrastructures. More than a mere legislative safeguard, the GDPR stands as a profound testament to the EU's commitment to fostering global norms and standards within the daunting digital landscape.

Furthermore, India's initiatives offer a noteworthy perspective on aspirations for technological sovereignty. By prioritizing domestic production and innovation, this initiative aims to strengthen industrial capabilities across various sectors, aligning with the overarching vision of reducing import reliance and enhancing technological self-sufficiency. The examination of these diverse global case studies unveils that the pursuit of technological autonomy is shaped by a complex tapestry of economic, political, and strategic factors, yielding invaluable lessons for policymakers and stakeholders navigating the intricate labyrinth of modern tech diplomacy.

Challenges in Achieving Technological Sovereignty

The pursuit of technological sovereignty unveils a myriad of complex challenges interwoven with economic, political, and security paradigms. Principal among these challenges is the pervasive dependence on foreign technology, especially within critical infrastructure and strategic sectors. Such reliance raises significant concerns regarding vulnerabilities and a nation's capacity to maintain control over essential systems during crises (Lungu et al., 2005). Moreover, the rapid pace of technological evolution complicates initiatives aimed at preempting emerging threats while safeguarding autonomy.

The intricate fabric of the global economy introduces further complexity, as supply chains often span multiple nations, rendering disengagement from international dependencies a daunting task fraught with the potential to disrupt established trade relations (Beck U et al., 2014). The asymmetrical distribution of technological capabilities among nations exacerbates this challenge, creating disparities in the pursuit of sovereignty and necessitating concerted efforts to bridge these gaps for a more equitable distribution of power.

The evolving landscape of cybersecurity threats compounds these issues. The increasing sophistication of malicious actors intensifies the difficulties surrounding the protection of national technological sovereignty. Striking a harmonious balance between pursuing independence and reaping the benefits of collaboration and knowledge exchange remains a significant obstacle. Navigating this multifaceted terrain requires intricate diplomacy and shrewd strategic maneuvers.

A nuanced balancing act is essential to foster innovation while simultaneously leveraging global talent and safeguarding national interests. Ethical considerations regarding data privacy, surveillance, and the responsible advancement of emerging technologies further complicate the endeavor of achieving technological sovereignty. These intertwined challenges underscore the intricate nature of securing and maintaining technological sovereignty within an interconnected global context, amplifying the need for comprehensive strategies to tackle the complexities of the digital age.

Impact of Global Supply Chains on National Security

In today's intricately interconnected landscape, global supply chains are indelibly linked to national security. Relying on international networks to source essential components and technologies introduces vulnerabilities while concurrently offering avenues for resilience (Vanhaute et al.). As nations grow increasingly dependent on diverse inputs from varied regions, the potentially severe repercussions of supply chain disruptions on national security have escalated markedly.

The integration of global supply chains across critical sectors—including technology, defense, and infrastructure—exacerbates the necessity of assessing and mitigating the risks tied to these dependencies. The interdependence among nations fuels concerns over the potential for exploitation, sabotage, or coercion stemming from supply chain disruptions (Carrillo R et al., 2021). A singular point of failure within a supply chain connected to essential defense systems could expose a nation to strategic vulnerabilities, significantly undermining its security posture.

As far as global supply chains are concerned, traditional paradigms of security and sovereignty fracture and reconstitute themselves in unexpected ways. Nations find their destinies inexorably intertwined through byzantine networks of technological codependence while policymakers grapple with an unprecedented calculus of risk and reward. These sprawling supply chains - simultaneously robust and fragile, efficient yet vulnerable - pulse with the lifeblood of modern economies. Their tendrils reach deep into the bedrock of national security, where military readiness and technological supremacy hang precariously in the balance. Strategic planners, confronting this new reality, must navigate a landscape where a disruption in a seemingly insignificant semiconductor facility halfway across the globe can cascade into a crisis of national proportion. The governance of these labyrinthine systems demands an almost prescient understanding of their manifold complexities - a challenge that defies conventional wisdom and demands radical new approaches to sovereignty in our hyperconnected age.

Beyond these associated risks, global supply chains also provide opportunities for enhancing national security through increased collaboration, diversification, and innovation. By pinpointing critical nodes and potential vulnerabilities within their networks, governments can devise strategies to mitigate risks, strengthen domestic capabilities, forge trusted partnerships, and promote secure, resilient networks. The application of emergent technologies—such as blockchain, artificial intelligence, and predictive analytics—can further enrich visibility and traceability throughout supply chains, augmenting security and risk management.

As the dynamics of global supply chains evolve, nations must actively engage in comprehensive risk assessments, strategic planning, and collaborative initiatives to safeguard national security interests. Striking a balance between leveraging the advantages of global interdependence while mitigating inherent security risks is paramount in an era where supply chains fundamentally shape the geopolitical landscape.

Strategic Approaches to Enhance Tech Sovereignty

In our intricately interconnected global arena, technological sovereignty has emerged as a pivotal focus for nations striving to assert greater control over essential technologies and digital infrastructures. A comprehensive array of strategic approaches is requisite for fortifying tech sovereignty, encompassing diverse dimensions essential to technological autonomy and national security.

A foundational strategy revolves around nurturing indigenous innovation and capabilities across critical technological sectors. This objective necessitates substantial investments in research and development, education, and entrepreneurship to cultivate a robust ecosystem characterized by domestic expertise and proprietary technologies (Center for Control A and Non-Proliferation, 2009). Encouraging domestic enterprises and startups to concentrate on strategic domains—such as telecommunications, cybersecurity, and emerging technologies—can significantly bolster a nation's capacity to diminish dependence on foreign sources and enhance its technological sovereignty.

Additionally, fostering strategic partnerships among government, academia, and industry plays an indispensable role in reinforcing tech sovereignty. Collaborative initiatives centered on knowledge sharing, joint research endeavors, and technology transfer can expedite the development of indigenous capabilities while alleviating potential vulnerabilities linked to reliance on external technology providers (Ajis et al., 2009). Moreover, establishing a favorable regulatory and policy environment that nurtures innovation, safeguards intellectual property, and promotes fair competition is crucial for cultivating a vibrant ecosystem conducive to technological self-sufficiency.

Furthermore, ensuring the diversification and security of supply chains through targeted investments in critical infrastructure and resources is paramount to enhancing a nation's resilience against disruptions while guaranteeing continuous access to indispensable technologies. This strategy may involve the strategic stockpiling of crucial components, bolstering local manufacturing capabilities, and building resilient supply chain networks that reduce dependencies on potentially adversarial nations or entities.

Advocating for international norms and standards that uphold the principles of technological sovereignty creates avenues for constructive engagement and cooperation among nations. By actively participating in multilateral forums, diplomatic initiatives, and trade agreements centered around data governance, technology transfer, and intellectual property rights, nations can collectively foster a global environment that respects each state's right to secure its technological interests.

Ultimately, a holistic approach to enhancing tech sovereignty necessitates a delicate equilibrium between championing innovation and economic growth while safeguarding national security interests. Through the implementation of comprehensive strategies that cultivate domestic expertise, forge collaborative partnerships, reinforce supply chain resilience, and advocate for international regulations, nations can adeptly navigate the intricate complexities of the digital era and strengthen their technological sovereignty amid an increasingly interconnected world.

Policy Frameworks and International Cooperation

As nations pursue technological sovereignty, there is an escalating recognition of the vital importance of robust policy frameworks and international collaboration (Beck U et al., 2014). The intricately interconnected nature of global technology ecosystems necessitates collective actions to address emerging challenges and establish common standards that foster both security and innovation.

At the national level, policymakers face the pressing challenge of crafting comprehensive strategies that encompass regulatory measures, investments in research and development, and the cultivation of indigenous technological capabilities. Additionally, international cooperation is crucial for harmonizing diverse approaches to technological sovereignty (Anghem et al., 1970). Multilateral forums and agreements provide essential platforms for dialogue and alignment of objectives, facilitating the creation of uniform standards and guidelines.

As digital technologies increasingly transcend borders, fostering a shared understanding and mutually beneficial collaboration becomes imperative to mitigate conflicts arising from divergent regulatory frameworks. Incentivizing responsible technology development and deployment is a core component of effective policy frameworks. This entails creating an environment where ethical considerations, transparency, and accountability are ingrained within industry practices. Mechanisms that promote compliance with international norms can encourage adherence to ethical principles governing technology.

Furthermore, proactive engagement in shaping international regulations and norms is vital for nations striving to assert their technological sovereignty. Participation in international organizations and diplomatic initiatives enables countries to influence the formulation of rules governing cyberspace and emerging technologies (Beck U et al., 2014). By actively involving themselves in global discussions about technology governance, nations can steer international cooperation towards a more equitable and secure technological ecosystem.

Establishing bilateral and multilateral partnerships focused on technology development and innovation can enhance individual countries' capabilities while fortifying collective resilience against external dependencies and vulnerabilities. Through joint research, knowledge exchange, and capacity-building initiatives, nations can leverage each other's strengths and expertise, fostering a collaborative environment that nurtures innovation while safeguarding national security interests.

As nations navigate the complexities associated with technological sovereignty, inclusive and transparent engagement among stakeholders at both national and international levels remains crucial. This ethos of cooperation and consensus-building serves as a foundation for devising effective policy frameworks and promoting international collaboration (Anghem et al., 1970). Ultimately, cultivating a global environment conducive to sustainable and secure technological advancement necessitates concerted efforts and principled engagement, emphasizing the significance of policy frameworks and international cooperation in the context of technological sovereignty.

Future Trends in Technological Sovereignty

As the global landscape continues to evolve, future trends in technological sovereignty are poised to transform paradigms of international relations and national security. Notably, there is a growing prioritization of indigenous innovation and research and development (R&D) initiatives aimed at achieving technological autonomy. Countries are directing substantial investments toward cutting-edge technologies while fostering their intellectual property rights to mitigate reliance on external sources, thereby safeguarding critical infrastructure and sensitive information (Curtis et al., 2016).

The rise of disruptive technologies—such as quantum computing, advanced artificial intelligence, and biotechnology—is set to further redefine the concept of technological sovereignty. Governments and industry leaders are closely monitoring these advancements to formulate robust strategies that align with national interests while also addressing the ethical considerations associated with their deployment.

Moreover, the convergence of technology and geopolitics represents another pivotal trend where the quest for technological leadership intersects with traditional power dynamics. This intersection underscores the necessity for tech diplomacy and proactive engagement with international allies to develop regulatory frameworks and standards for emerging technologies (Grevi et al., 2020). The evolving landscape of cyber threats and hybrid warfare accentuates the urgency for nations to strengthen their cyber defenses and cultivate resilient digital ecosystems. Collaborative initiatives aimed at establishing transnational norms and protocols for cyber operations are expected to gain traction within the domain of tech sovereignty.

Additionally, future trends in technological sovereignty will likely involve a reassessment of trade and supply chain dynamics, particularly in crucial sectors such as telecommunications, semiconductors, and national infrastructure. The push for supply chain diversification and self-sufficiency in strategic technologies reflects a heightened focus on mitigating vulnerabilities and ensuring continuity amid geopolitical uncertainties. At the same time, ethical dimensions will remain at the forefront, fueling discussions on responsible innovation, data privacy, and respect for human rights in the application of advanced technologies.

In conclusion, the trajectory of technological sovereignty is characterized by the dynamic interplay of innovation, security imperatives, and diplomatic efforts. Proactively adapting to these forthcoming trends is essential for nations as they navigate the complex interdependencies of the digital age, asserting their roles as custodians of technological progress while safeguarding national interests.

Conclusion: Balancing Innovation and Security

As the world becomes increasingly interconnected through technology, the notion of technological sovereignty has emerged as a critical concern for nations aiming to strike a delicate balance between fostering innovation and maintaining security. This chapter has explored the multifaceted future trends in technological sovereignty, illuminating the intricate and dynamic landscape that governments, corporations, and international organizations must skillfully navigate to maintain control over their technological capabilities (Curtis et al., 2016). The paramount importance of this complex balancing act cannot be overstated, as it profoundly influences a nation's competitive edge in the global arena and its fundamental capacity to protect critical infrastructure and safeguard sensitive data.

Achieving a harmonious equilibrium between fostering groundbreaking innovation and protecting vital national interests demands a sophisticated, multifaceted strategy. This encompasses proactive and substantial investment in cutting-edge research and development to diminish reliance on external technologies and enhance national technological autonomy (Lungu et al., 2005). Furthermore, the cultivation of robust public-private partnerships can catalyze the strategic alignment of innovation trajectories with pressing national security imperatives.

In this rapidly evolving technological landscape, regulatory frameworks must demonstrate unprecedented adaptability to address emerging threats within the digital ecosystem while avoiding the stifling of technological advancement. International collaboration emerges as an absolutely paramount consideration, necessitating sustained dialogue and meaningful cooperation across borders to collectively secure increasingly complex technological infrastructures (Curtis et al., 2016).

However, striking the optimal equilibrium between innovation and security presents formidable challenges. Overly restrictive controls may inadvertently impede innovation and economic growth (Lungu et al., 2005). Moreover, the breathtaking pace of technological evolution introduces additional layers of complexity, demanding continuous vigilance and adaptability. Global supply chains, while indispensable for technological advancement, simultaneously introduce critical security vulnerabilities and dependencies.

The convergence of these multifaceted factors underscores the urgent need for nuanced strategies that acknowledge and address inherent tensions. Embracing an agile and adaptive approach to technological sovereignty becomes vital for nations seeking to respond effectively to the rapidly evolving landscapes of security and technology. As we peer into the future, achieving this delicate balance will require unprecedented levels of collaboration and unwavering commitment from all stakeholders—governments, industry players, and international organizations alike. Only through a profound shared sense of responsibility can we effectively navigate the critical intersection of innovation and security, ultimately shaping a future where technological sovereignty becomes synonymous with global resilience and transformative progress.

References:

- Curtis, Simon, 2016, https://core.ac.uk/download/41993290.pdf
- Grevi, Giovanni, 2020, https://core.ac.uk/download/323112026.pdf
- Dahan, Michael, "Murdoch University", 2012, https://core.ac.uk/download/pdf/12237606.pdf
- Cottey, Andrew, Csernatoni, Raluca, Dobber, Jeroen, Fiott, Daniel, Ghalehdar, Payam, Groitl, Gerlinde, Martill, Benjamin, "LSE Ideas", 2022, https://core.ac.uk/download/511316322.pdf
- Jan Gunnarsson, 2024, https://core.ac.uk/download/pdf/7051611.pdf
- Lungu, Sorin., 2005, https://core.ac.uk/download/5076087.pdf
- Beck U., Bevir M., Bevir M., Bril L.-V., CBRN CoE Newsletter, Coker C., Council, Deutsch K., Dupré B., Dupré B., Ellul J., European Commission, European Commission, European Commission, European Parliament and the Council, Giddens A., Kamil Zwolski, Kaunert C., Kirchner E., Kirchner E., Krahmann E., Mignone A., Rathbun B.C., Rhodes R.A.W., Rosenau J.N., Schmidt K., Schroeder U.C., Sperling J.A., Stoker G., Von Stein J., Weber M., Winfield G., "'Informa UK Limited'", 2014,
- Kvaleberg, Ola, Lexau, Sander, "'Saint Louis University'",

2024, https://core.ac.uk/download/617933119.pdf

- Fosca Giannotti, Francesca Pratesi, giovanni comande, Salvatore Ruggieri, 2021, https://core.ac.uk/download/559257952.pdf

- Ajis, Mohd Na'eim, Keling, Mohamad Faisol, Shuib, Md. Shukri, "'Canadian Center of Science and Education'", 2009, https://core.ac.uk/download/12122068.pdf

- Anghem, Henric, Engstrand, Linus, "Duke University School of Law", 1970, https://core.ac.uk/download/62551378.pdf

- Vanhaute, Eric, 2024, https://core.ac.uk/download/pdf/6584464.pdf

- Robles Carrillo, Margarita, "'Elsevier BV'", 2021, https://core.ac.uk/download/479173631.pdf

12

THE FUTURE OF TECHPLOMACY: CHALLENGES AND OPPORTUNITIES

Emerging Trends in Techplomacy

IN THE RAPIDLY METAMORPHOSING sphere of international affairs, the amalgamation of technology and diplomacy has ushered in an unprecedented era replete with complex interconnections and exceptional challenges. As we embark on an exploration of techplomacy, it is imperative to delineate the predominant trends that are sculpting the global governance landscape of technological advancements (Alfarizi, B.Z., Silvyasari, D., & Heryadi, D. 2024). A cornerstone of this exploration is the recognition of how emergent technologies are reshaping diplomatic agendas and readjusting the balance of power among nations. The meteoric rise of digital platforms, the advent of artificial intelligence (AI), and the escalation of cyber warfare have introduced an array of complexities, necessitating a sagacious examination of their repercussions on conventional diplomatic paradigms (Alfarizi, B.Z., Silvyasari, D., & Heryadi, D. 2024)

Within these burgeoning trends, the concept of data sovereignty has emerged as a significant preoccupation, compelling governments to recalibrate their strategies to protect national interests in the digital sphere. Furthermore, the increasing prominence of technological magnates as crucial actors in international relations has instigated intricate negotiations and assertive positions regarding privacy, cybersecurity, and the ethical utilization of fledgling technologies (Alfarizi, B.Z., Silvyasari, D., & Heryadi, D. 2024). The evolving landscape of techplomacy calls for a nuanced analysis of the dynamic interplay between innovation and diplomacy, elucidating the inherent tensions and synergies that characterize this convoluted relationship. Additionally, the expansion of digital diplomacy has reconfigured communication and engagement modalities among states, heralding a new epoch in which policy decisions are influenced not solely by geopolitical imperatives but also by technological requirements (Alfarizi, B.Z., Silvyasari, D., & Heryadi, D. 2024).

As nations endeavor to harness the potential of avant-garde technologies, they are confronted with the urgent challenge of mitigating adverse outcomes, which range from disinformation campaigns to vulnerabilities in critical infrastructure (Alfarizi et al., 2024; Putra et al., 2024). The impact of social media on public perception and the dissemination of information has surfaced as a paramount facet of contemporary techplomacy, necessitating an astute understanding of the nexus between digital discourse and diplomatic strategies. In this milieu, the confluence of technology and diplomacy assumes unprecedented significance, impelling practitioners and stakeholders to navigate multifarious challenges and complexities (Alfarizi, B.Z., Silvyasari, D., & Heryadi, D. 2024). Only by deftly situating these emergent trends within the broader context of global affairs can we glean the comprehensive implications of techplomacy, thereby offering profound insights into the future trajectories of international relations.

Challenges Posed by Rapid Technological Advancements

The swift advancements in technology have engendered a period marked by unparalleled connectivity and innovation, yet they have simultaneously unveiled a myriad of intricate challenges for contemporary diplomacy. At the forefront of these challenges is the rapid pace of technological evolution, often eclipsing the capacity of regulatory frameworks and international agreements to adapt effectively(Alfarizi et al., 2024). This predicament poses a formidable obstacle as diplomatic endeavors grapple with burgeoning issues such as data privacy, cybersecurity, and the ethical implications of disruptive technologies(Alfarizi et al., 2024; Sun et al., 2024).

Moreover, the global nature of these technological advancements can exacerbate existing geopolitical frictions as nations vie for supremacy in pioneering sectors such as artificial intelligence and quantum computing (Alfarizi et al., 2024). The potential for escalating cyber confrontations and the militarization of technology further complicates the multifaceted dilemmas faced by diplomats navigating this swiftly changing terrain. Another pressing challenge is the inequitable distribution of technological benefits across different regions and populations. While developed nations and technological hubs thrive in the bounty of progress, numerous areas lag significantly behind, thereby exacerbating the digital divide (Alfarizi et al., 2024; Putra et al., 2024). This disparity not only cultivates economic and social inequities but also engenders diplomatic quandaries in fostering inclusive and collaborative global relations.

Additionally, the rampant proliferation of misinformation and disinformation via technological platforms has placed unprecedented strain on diplomatic endeavors, necessitating the formulation of innovative and agile responses to counteract the amplification of falsehoods and the erosion of trust among nations(Alfarizi et al., 2024; Putra et al., 2024). The intricate interplay between technology and conventional power dynamics presents further obstacles for techplomacy. As technological conglomerates exert considerable influence over global narratives, their actions and decisions frequently intertwine with geopolitical interests, blurring the lines between public and private governance (Alfarizi et al., 2024; Sun et al., 2024).

Navigating this intricate tapestry of corporate interests, state sovereignty, and international norms becomes increasingly convoluted, demanding that diplomats adapt and devise novel strategies to maintain equilibrium. Ultimately, the sprightly cadence of technological upheaval necessitates that diplomats anticipate and mitigate the potential fallout from rapid changes while striving to uphold international laws and norms that struggle to keep pace with the frenetic tempo of innovation(Alfarizi et al., 2024). Addressing these multifaceted challenges requires a strategic and collaborative approach to techplomacy grounded in foresight, inclusivity, and concerted global cooperation(Alfarizi et al., 2024; Sun, et al., 2024).

The Rising Importance of Policy Frameworks and International Collaboration

As nations pursue technological sovereignty, there is an escalating recognition of the vital importance of robust policy frameworks and international collaboration (Beck U et al., 2014). The intricately interconnected nature of global technology ecosystems necessitates collective actions to address emerging challenges and establish common standards that foster both security and innovation.

At the national level, policymakers face the pressing challenge of crafting comprehensive strategies that encompass regulatory measures, investments in research and development, and the cultivation of indigenous technological capabilities. Additionally, international cooperation is crucial for harmonizing diverse approaches to technological sovereignty (Anghem et al., 1970). Multilateral forums and agreements provide essential platforms for dialogue and alignment of objectives, facilitating the creation of uniform standards and guidelines.

As digital technologies increasingly transcend borders, fostering a shared understanding and mutually beneficial collaboration becomes imperative to mitigate conflicts arising from divergent regulatory frameworks. Incentivizing responsible technology development and deployment is a core component of effective policy frameworks. This entails creating an environment where ethical considerations, transparency, and accountability are ingrained within industry practices. Mechanisms that promote compliance with international norms can encourage adherence to ethical principles governing technology.

Furthermore, proactive engagement in shaping international regulations and norms is vital for nations striving to assert their technological sovereignty. Participation in international organizations and diplomatic initiatives enables countries to influence the formulation of rules governing cyberspace and emerging technologies (Beck U et al., 2014). By actively involving themselves in global discussions about technology governance, nations can steer international cooperation towards a more equitable and secure technological ecosystem.

Establishing bilateral and multilateral partnerships focused on technology development and innovation can enhance individual countries' capabilities while fortifying collective resilience against external dependencies and vulnerabilities. Through joint research, knowledge exchange, and capacity-building initiatives, nations can leverage each other's strengths and expertise, fostering a collaborative environment that nurtures innovation while safeguarding national security interests.

As nations navigate the complexities associated with technological sovereignty, inclusive and transparent engagement among stakeholders at both national and international levels remains crucial. This ethos of cooperation and consensus-building serves as a foundation for devising effective policy frameworks and promoting international collaboration (Anghem et al., 1970). Ultimately, cultivating a global environment conducive to sustainable and secure technological advancement necessitates concerted efforts and principled engagement, emphasizing the significance of policy frameworks and international cooperation in the context of technological sovereignty.

Future Trends in Technological Sovereignty

As the global landscape continues to evolve, future trends in technological sovereignty are poised to transform paradigms of international relations and national security. Notably, there is a growing prioritization of indigenous innovation and research and development (R&D) initiatives aimed at achieving technological autonomy. Countries are directing substantial investments toward cutting-edge technologies while fostering their intellectual property rights to mitigate reliance on external sources, thereby safeguarding critical infrastructure and sensitive information (Curtis et al., 2016).

The rise of disruptive technologies—such as quantum computing, advanced artificial intelligence, and biotechnology—is set to further redefine the concept of technological sovereignty. Governments and industry leaders are closely monitoring these advancements to formulate robust strategies that align with national interests while also addressing the ethical considerations associated with their deployment.

Moreover, the convergence of technology and geopolitics represents another pivotal trend where the quest for technological leadership intersects with traditional power dynamics. This intersection underscores the necessity for tech diplomacy and proactive engagement with international allies to develop regulatory frameworks and standards for emerging technologies (Grevi et al., 2020). The evolving landscape of cyber threats and hybrid warfare accentuates the urgency for nations to strengthen their cyber defenses and cultivate resilient digital ecosystems. Collaborative initiatives aimed at establishing transnational norms and protocols for cyber operations are expected to gain traction within the realm of tech sovereignty.

Additionally, future trends in technological sovereignty will likely involve a reassessment of trade and supply chain dynamics, particularly in crucial sectors such as telecommunications, semiconductors, and national infrastructure. The push for supply chain diversification and self-sufficiency in strategic technologies reflects a heightened focus on mitigating vulnerabilities and ensuring continuity amid geopolitical uncertainties. At the same time, ethical dimensions will remain at the forefront, fueling discussions on responsible innovation, data privacy, and respect for human rights in the application of advanced technologies.

In conclusion, the trajectory of technological sovereignty is characterized by the dynamic interplay of innovation, security imperatives, and diplomatic efforts. Proactively adapting to these forthcoming trends is essential for nations as they navigate the complex interdependencies of the digital age, asserting their roles as custodians of technological progress while safeguarding national interests.

Balancing Innovation and Security

As the world becomes increasingly interconnected through technology, the notion of technological sovereignty has emerged as a critical concern for nations aiming to strike a balance between innovation and security. This chapter has explored future trends in technological sovereignty, illuminating the intricate landscape that governments, corporations, and international organizations must navigate to maintain control over their technological capabilities (Curtis et al., 2016). The importance of this balancing act cannot be overstated, as it influences not only a nation's competitive edge in the global arena but also its capacity to protect critical infrastructure and safeguard sensitive data.

Achieving a harmonious balance between fostering innovation and protecting national interests necessitates a multifaceted strategy. This includes proactive investment in research and development to reduce reliance on external technologies and enhance national technological autonomy (Lungu et al., 2005). Additionally, promoting strong public-private partnerships can facilitate the alignment of innovation with national security imperatives.

Regulatory frameworks must adapt to emerging threats within the digital ecosystem without stifling technological advancement. International collaboration is paramount, requiring dialogue and cooperation across borders to collectively secure technological infrastructures (Curtis et al., 2016).

However, striking the right equilibrium between innovation and security presents its own challenges. Stricter controls may impede innovation and economic growth (Lungu et al., 2005). Moreover, the rapid pace of technological evolution introduces further complexities, necessitating continuous vigilance and adaptability. Global supply chains, while essential for technological advancement, also pose security vulnerabilities and dependencies.

The convergence of these factors highlights the need for nuanced strategies that recognize and address inherent tensions. Embracing an agile and adaptive approach to technological sovereignty is vital for nations to respond effectively to the evolving landscapes of security and technology. As we look ahead, achieving this delicate balance will require ongoing collaboration and commitment from all stakeholders—governments, industry players, and international organizations alike. Only through a shared sense of responsibility can we effectively navigate the intersection of innovation and security, shaping a future where technological sovereignty is synonymous with global resilience and progress.

Policy Innovations and Regulatory Approaches

In the progressively evolving landscape of technology and diplomacy, the necessity for policy innovations and regulatory frameworks has become increasingly pronounced. As nations grapple with the implications of emerging technologies on global affairs, it is paramount to develop frameworks that strike a delicate balance between nurturing innovation and addressing potential risks and ethical considerations. The complexities of techplomacy prompt policymakers to adapt and evolve in tandem with technological advancements, necessitating agile and forward-thinking regulatory strategies. (Vasen, F. 2017).

A pivotal area of focus lies in establishing cross-border regulatory standards to govern the utilization and proliferation of emerging technologies. In a digital realm that transcends traditional geographical confines, harmonizing regulations across nations can facilitate smoother international cooperation and mitigate potential conflicts arising from disparate regulatory frameworks. (Ludlow, K., Bowman, D., Gatof, J., & Bennett, M. 2015). This calls for concerted endeavors in multilateral forums to draft cohesive policies accommodating the diverse interests and concerns of global stakeholders while aligning with overarching principles of responsible and ethical technological advancement.

Moreover, a critical facet of policy innovation involves achieving a delicate equilibrium between incentivizing technological progress and safeguarding national security and individual rights. This requires formulating nuanced regulatory measures that promote innovation and entrepreneurship within a framework of accountability and transparency. Policymakers must navigate the intricacies of regulating cutting-edge technologies such as artificial intelligence, biotechnology, and quantum computing, accounting for geopolitical implications, ethical considerations, and the imperative to ensure compatibility with existing legal and ethical norms. (Ludlow, K., Bowman, D., Gatof, J., & Bennett, M. 2015).

Furthermore, the emergence of techplomacy necessitates a reevaluation of traditional diplomatic protocols, incorporating technology-specific expertise into diplomatic missions. The convergence of technology and diplomacy underscores the need for diplomats and foreign policy practitioners to possess profound insights into technological intricacies, enabling effective engagement in shaping regulations and policies that link diplomatic relationships with technological breakthroughs.

Another vital domain for policy innovation revolves around fostering public-private partnerships to jointly tackle regulatory challenges and leverage technological opportunities. Engaging with tech companies, research institutions, and civil society enables a holistic approach to regulatory design, drawing upon a spectrum of perspectives and expertise to create robust and adaptive frameworks. Such collaborative efforts enhance the inclusivity and efficacy of regulatory initiatives while fostering an environment conducive to responsible innovation and global cooperation. (Vasen, F. (2017).

Stakeholders must adopt a forward-thinking mindset in navigating the convoluted terrain of policy innovations and regulatory approaches. They must acknowledge that regulatory frameworks must remain agile and adaptable to accommodate the rapid evolution of technology and its impact on international relations. Embracing interdisciplinary dialogue and proactive engagement with diverse stakeholders will be vital in shaping regulatory approaches that harness technology's transformative potential while upholding the values of global cooperation, ethics, and security.

Addressing Ethical Concerns in Global Tech Governance

Ethical concerns have emerged as critical considerations for policymakers, industry leaders, and international organizations within the swiftly evolving global tech governance domain. As nations grapple with technology's escalating influence on socio-economic landscapes, addressing ethical dilemmas becomes paramount in shaping a responsible and sustainable framework for technomancy.

One of the foremost ethical issues pertains to data privacy and protection. With the proliferation of digital information and the application of sophisticated data analytics, safeguarding individual privacy rights and ensuring the secure management of sensitive data has become a central challenge. Striking the delicate balance between innovation and privacy mandates comprehensive regulatory architectures and proactive policy interventions that prioritize the ethical utilization of data while fostering technological progress (Verma, J. 2023 Stahl, B. 2013).

Furthermore, ethical considerations extend to the application of emerging technologies such as artificial intelligence (AI), biotechnology, and quantum computing. These avant-garde innovations possess immense potential to transform various industries and global systems; however, their ethical implications necessitate careful navigation. Inquiries regarding AI ethics, encompassing algorithmic biases, transparency in decision-making, and the societal impacts of automation, require rigorous ethical appraisals and international collaboration to establish standards promoting responsible AI deployment. (Stahl, B. 2013).

Moreover, advancements in biotechnology and gene editing present moral quandaries concerning human enhancement, genetic manipulation, and the boundaries of scientific experimentation. Addressing these concerns in an inclusive global manner necessitates interdisciplinary dialogues, ethical guidelines, and normative protocols that align technological progress with ethical imperatives. (Verma, J. 2023; Stahl, B. 2013).

Additionally, the ethical dimensions of tech governance are intricately linked to issues of digital inclusion and equitable access. Bridging the digital divide and ensuring equal opportunities for technological participation constitute urgent ethical endeavors in nurturing global techplomacy. By prioritizing digital literacy initiatives, advancing universal connectivity, and fostering an environment of inclusivity, nations can pursue ethical tech governance that empowers diverse populations and mitigates disparities.

Ultimately, addressing ethical concerns in global tech governance demands collaborative undertakings among governments, industry, civil society, and academia. This collective approach should focus on establishing ethical principles, and promoting transparency while bolstering accountability within the tech-plomacy framework, thereby sculpting a future where technological advancements are guided by ethical considerations and contribute positively to global prosperity. (Stahl, B. 2013).

Case Studies: Successful Techplomacy Initiatives

In examining successful instances of techplomacy, one discerns that a strategic amalgamation of innovation, diplomacy, and technological acumen has yielded impactful global initiatives. One compelling exemplification involves the collaborative engagement between leading tech companies and international organizations aimed at addressing pressing global challenges. Through partnerships with entities such as the United Nations and its specialized agencies, tech firms have significantly contributed to sustainable development goals, disaster response efforts, and facilitating access to education and healthcare in underserved regions.

Another noteworthy instance is the establishment of cross-border data-sharing arrangements designed to foster international cooperation while simultaneously safeguarding privacy and security. Diplomatic negotiation and coordination paved the way for frameworks that balance the imperatives of data-driven innovation with the necessity to protect individual rights and national interests. These collaborations serve as paradigms of successful techplomacy, wherein mutually beneficial outcomes are attained through transparent dialogue and consensus-building. (Royo, S., Pina, V., & Garcia-Rayado, J. 2020)

Moreover, the deployment of digital infrastructure in conflict-prone regions has illustrated the potential for technology to act as a catalyst for peace and reconciliation. By harnessing innovative solutions, governments and tech stakeholders have actively bolstered initiatives to enhance connectivity, access to information, and communication channels, thereby contributing to conflict resolution and long-term stability. (Bandara, W., Syed, R., Ranathunga, B., & Kulathilaka, K. 2018). Such endeavors illuminate the transformative capacity of techplomacy in alleviating geopolitical tensions and fostering trust among disparate communities.

Additionally, tech ambassadors' proactive involvement in facilitating inclusive dialogues on emergent technologies has yielded significant outcomes in enhancing global understanding and cooperation. By convening summits, workshops, and platforms for knowledge exchange, these envoys have cultivated an environment conducive to sharing best practices, harmonizing regulatory approaches, and advocating for responsible innovation. This anticipatory approach epitomizes the critical role that tech diplomats play in shaping the future landscape of technology and diplomacy. (Bandara, W., Syed, R., Ranathunga, B., & Kulathilaka, K. 2018).

Finally, the coordinated responses to cybersecurity threats and initiatives aimed at enhancing resilience stand out as exemplary manifestations of successful techplomacy. As cyberattacks increasingly transcend national confines, cooperative efforts that merge technical prowess with diplomatic strategies become indispensable. Through joint cybersecurity initiatives, nations have collaborated to fortify digital defenses, establish early warning systems, and reinforce norms of responsible conduct in cyberspace. These case studies underscore the integral importance of techplomacy in tackling complex transnational dilemmas and the immense potential for fostering a positive global impact through inventive collaborations. (Royo, S., Pina, V., & Garcia-Rayado, J. 2020)

Forecasting Future Developments in Technology and Diplomacy

As we cast our gaze toward the horizon of technology and diplomacy, it becomes increasingly evident that the fabric of international relations will be intricately woven with the evolution of technological innovations. Several pivotal trends are poised to shape the future of techplomacy, as global dynamics remain influenced by rapid innovation and digital transformation. One of the foremost developments is the intersection of nascent technologies such as artificial intelligence, quantum computing, and biotechnology with diplomatic pursuits. The employment of these robust tools will not merely redefine conventional diplomatic strategies but will also unveil novel opportunities for engagement and conflict resolution. (Coates, V., Farooque, M., Klavans, R., Lapid, K., Linstone, H., Pistorius, C., & Porter, A. 2001).

Moreover, as nations endeavor to secure their positions within the digital domain, matters related to technological sovereignty and national security are likely to become focal points of diplomatic discourse. This trend may precipitate a reconfiguration of global power dynamics, with countries competing to assert their superiority in the technological sphere. Furthermore, the proliferation of data-driven decision-making processes and the advent of intelligent infrastructures will necessitate an evolution in diplomatic practices to adeptly manage the interconnectivity of societies and economies. (Kyebambe, M., Cheng, G., Huang, Y., He, C., & Zhang, Z. 2017).

Cybersecurity concerns will dominate the diplomatic landscape, demanding cooperative endeavors to fortify international frameworks and standards in response to evolving cyber threats. Additionally, the ethical dimensions of deploying and governing novel technologies will persist in influencing diplomatic agendas, prompting the formulation of standardized ethical guidelines and norms that transcend international boundaries. It is also imperative to anticipate the burgeoning role of public-private partnerships in techplomacy, wherein governments engage closely with tech corporations to leverage their expertise in addressing global challenges and fostering sustainable development. (Coates, V., Farooque, M., Klavans, R., Lapid, K., Linstone, H., Pistorius, C., & Porter, A. 2001).

Lastly, the increasing influence of non-state actors within the digital realm will propel a movement towards more inclusive diplomatic processes, incorporating a diverse array of stakeholders from civil society, academia, and the private sector. These prospective developments underscore the urgent necessity for diplomatic institutions to evolve and adapt in tandem with the rapid acceleration of technological innovation, charting a pathway for harmonious integration of technology and diplomacy in the forthcoming decades. (Kyebambe, M., Cheng, G., Huang, Y., He, C., & Zhang, Z. 2017).

Conclusive Insights: Paving the Way Forward

As we contemplate the future of techplomacy, it becomes increasingly evident that technology and diplomacy's intertwined essence will persist in profoundly impactful global affairs. The convergence of these two domains unveils both challenges and opportunities necessitating meticulous consideration and strategic foresight. Paving the way forward entails a united effort to traverse the complex landscape of emerging technologies and their implications for international relations.

A pivotal aspect involves the need for adaptable and prescient diplomatic strategies capable of effectively addressing these rapid technological advancements. Traditional paradigms of diplomacy must metamorphose to accommodate the complexities of the digital age, wherein issues such as cyber threats, data governance, and the ethical application of AI assume paramount significance. Diplomatic corps and foreign ministries should integrate technologically adept personnel possessing profound understandings of digital tools and platforms, ensuring that diplomatic missions remain relevant and effective amidst the shifting technological terrain.

Moreover, establishing collaborative frameworks and agreements to govern global tech governance will be essential in shaping the trajectory ahead. This necessitates a multilateral effort to cultivate common standards, regulations, and protocols that promote responsible innovation while guarding against the potential misuse of emerging technologies. By nurturing dialogue and cooperation among nations, a harmonized approach to tech governance can mitigate the risks of technological fragmentation and foster interoperability, thereby facilitating cross-border collaboration and trade.

In addition to regulatory considerations, it is crucial to acknowledge the vital role of public-private partnerships in influencing the course of techplomacy. By engaging with industry leaders, governments can leverage their expertise and resources to drive innovative solutions for shared challenges while fostering an environment conducive to sustainable technological advancement. By forging strategic alliances with technology firms, governments can harness collective intelligence to tackle transnational issues, from climate change and healthcare to cybersecurity and equitable digital access.

Ethical considerations stand prominently at the forefront of defining the future landscape of techplomacy. As technology continues to permeate various societal facets, critical ethical inquiries must be deliberated within the realm of international affairs. Dialogues surrounding data privacy, algorithmic biases, and AI ethics demand informed and inclusive discussions that incorporate diverse perspectives, ultimately crafting universally applicable ethical norms that uphold human rights and societal well-being.

Ultimately, the future of techplomacy hinges on the capacity to anticipate and adapt to the rapid technological transformations that lie ahead. Embracing a proactive stance toward technological innovations while remaining cognizant of their geopolitical and socio-economic implications will be pivotal in charting a course toward a more resilient, inclusive, and cooperative global order. By fostering a dynamic and responsive ecosystem for tech-enabled diplomacy, the international community can collaboratively navigate the challenges and seize the vast opportunities presented by the intersection of technology and diplomacy.

References

1. **A. Dutta.** "Multilateral Diplomacy: Role Of Brics In Altering The Discourse Of Global Governance." *International Journal of Scientific & Technology Research*, 8 (2019): 1026-1031.

2. **A. Kussainova.** "Optimization of the diplomatic service's activity in conditions of modern international relations and information technology." *Global Journal on Technology*, 4 (2013).

3. **A. A.** Alfarizi, Baqi Zaenulhaq, Deasy Silvyasari, and Dudy Heryadi. 2024. "Global Governance in the 21st Century: A Digital Trends and Transformation". *Global Local Interactions: Journal of International Relations* 4 (1):57-67. https://doi.org/10.22219/gli.v4i1.31682.

4. **B. Stahl.** "Ethical Issues of Emerging ICT Applications." (2013): 1349-1360. https://doi.org/10.4018/978-1-4666-3670-5.CH004.

5. **C. Weiss.** "How Do Science and Technology Affect International Affairs?." *Minerva*, 53 (2015): 411-430. https://doi.org/10.1007/S11024-015-9286-1.

6. **Chuanfeng Sun,** Guihuang Jiang, and Jingqiang Zhang. "An Analysis of Hotspots, Subject Structure, and Emerging Trends in Digital Governance Research." *Sage Open* (2024).

7. **C.** V. Coates, M. Farooque, R. Klavans, K. Lapid, H.

Linstone, C. Pistorius and A. Porter. "On the Future of Technological Forecasting." *Technological Forecasting and Social Change*, 67 (2001): 1-17. https://doi.org/10.1016/S0040-1625(00)00122-0.

8. **D. Bowman,** A. Karinne Ludlow, Jake Gatof, and Michael G. Bennett. "Regulating Emerging and Future Technologies in the Present." *NanoEthics*, 9 (2015): 151-163. https://doi.org/10.1007/S11569-015-0223-4.

9. **Ei, Austine,** Sunday On, Lizette Ne, Ugochi Aa, Jovita In, Amarachi Se, Eze Ud, Maureen Ua, Brian OO*, Ifeoma Bu, Loveth Ie, Mercy An, Nneoma No, Ngozi Ao, and Nkeiruka Go. "Assessment of the Learning Management Systems in Tertiary Institutions in Nigeria: A Narrative Review of Published Studies from 2008 to 2024." *Nursing & Healthcare International Journal* (2024).

10. **Federico Vasen.** "Responsible Innovation in Developing Countries: An Enlarged Agenda." (2017): 93-109. https://doi.org/10.1007/978-3-319-64834-7_6.

11. **Grover, Stephanie A.,** Christine J. Williams, Adrienne Co-Dyre, David Malkin, Jim Whitlock, and on behalf of the ACCESS consortium. "Abstract B069: ACCESS: Advancing childhood cancer experience, science, and survivorship in Canada." *Cancer Research* (2024).

12. **I. Kunina.** "Network Aspect of Multilateral Diplomacy." *Nauchnyi dialog* (2022). https://doi.org/10.24224/2227-1295-2022-11-9-392-409.

13. **J. Verma.** "Ethical Concerns for the Global Technological Societies: Some Observations." *Mind and Society* (2023). https://doi.org/10.56011/mind-mri-122-20231.

14. **K. T. Alekseeva,** Lie Khyonh Ti and Hoang Thi Kieu Trinh. "MULTILATERAL DIPLOMACY IN THE XXI CENTURY: NEW FORMS, PROBLEMS AND PROSPECTS IN COOPERATION WITH INTERNATIONAL ORGANIZATIONS." *Herald UNU. International Economic Relations And World Economy* (2021). https://doi.org/10.32782/2413-9971/2021-39-2.

15. **Mashiah, Itzhak.** (2023). Tech-Diplomacy: High-Tech Driven Rhetoric to Shape National Reputation.

16. **Meryem Marzouki.** Techplomacy: Innovative Diplomatic Practice or Highest Stage of Neoliberalism in Global Digital Governance? 2021 IPSA World Congress, International Political Science Association, Jul 2021, Lisbon, Portugal. ⟨halshs-03098852⟩.

17. **Moses Ntanda Kyebambe,** Ge Cheng, Y. Huang, Chunhui He, and Zhenyu Zhang. "Forecasting emerging technologies: A supervised learning approach through patent analysis." *Technological Forecasting and Social Change*, 125 (2017): 236-244. https://doi.org/10.1016/J.TECHFORE.2017.08.002.

18. **Pavlina Ittelson,** Martin Rauchbauer. "Tech diplomacy practice in the San Francisco Bay Area." *Diplo* (2023).

19. **Putra, Chandra Anugrah,** Ade Salahudin Permadi, and Muhammad Andi Setiawan. "Information technology innovation in sports learning: understanding global trends and challenges." *Retos* (2024): n. pag.

20. **S. Royo,** V. Pina, and Jaime Garcia-Rayado. "Decide Madrid: A Critical Analysis of an Award-Winning e-Participation Initiative." *Sustainability* (2020). https://doi.

org/10.3390/su12041674.

21. **W. Bandara, R. Syed,** Bandula Ranathunga, and K. Kulathilaka. "People-Centric, ICT-Enabled Process Innovations via Community, Public and Private Sector Partnership, and e-Leadership: The Case of the Dompe eHospital in Sri Lanka." (2018): 125-148. https://doi.org/10.1007/978-3-319-58307-5_8.

BIBLIOGRAPHY

Aboy, M., Brongersma, M., Cohen, I. G., De Jong, E., Floridi, L., Gasser, U., Kop, M., Laflamme, R., Minssen, T., & Quintel, T. (2023). Global governance in the 21st century: A digital trends and transformation. *Global Local Interactions: Journal of International Relations*, 4(1), 57-67. https://doi.org/10.22 219/gli.v4i1.31682

A. Dutta. (2019). Multilateral diplomacy: Role of BRICS in altering the discourse of global governance. *International Journal of Scientific & Technology Research*, 8, 1026-1031.

A. Kussainova. (2013). Optimization of the diplomatic service's activity in conditions of modern international relations and information technology. *Global Journal on Technology*, 4.

ALAVI, S.-H. R. (2023). [Title]. https://core.ac.uk/downloa d/596363383.pdf (URL assumed)

Amoretti, F., & Santaniello, M. (2015). *Universidad Católica de Colombia. Facultad de Derecho.* https://core.ac.uk/downlo ad/213561036.pdf

Antonio Lopez. (2008). The MacArthur Foundation digital media and learning initiative. https://core.ac.uk/download/7 1339822.pdf

Bajwa, A. (2021). Role of technology in international affairs. New Delhi: Pentagon Press.

Becker-Jakob, U. (2011). Notions of justice in the hopeful paradigms of urban justice expansion in Germany. *Frankfurt am Main*. https://www.ssoar.info/ssoar/bitstream/document/45531/3/ssoar-2011-becker-jakob-Notions_of_Justice_in_the.pdf

Berry, P. M., Brown, I., Everard, M., Firbank, L. G., Harrison, P. A., Lundy, L., Quine, C. P., Rowan, J. S., Wade, R., & Watts, K. (2015). [Title]. https://core.ac.uk/download/141567357.pdf

Beck, U., Bevir, M., Bril, L.-V., Coker, C., Deutsch, K., Dupré, B., Ellul, J., et al. (2014). *Informa UK Limited*.

Bourne, C. D., & Edwards, L. (2021). [Title]. *De Gruyter Mouton*. https://core.ac.uk/download/372706712.pdf

Bowman, C. (2021). [Title]. *JMU Scholarly Commons*. https://core.ac.uk/download/519862893.pdf

Burke, L. H. (2012). *Ambassador at large: Diplomat extraordinary*. Springer Science & Business Media.

Burri, M., Christen, M., Elger, B., Hauser, C., Ienca, M., Loi, M., Schneble, C., Shaw, D. E., & Vigano, E. (2022). [Title]. https://www.zora.uzh.ch/id/eprint/225228/1/SSRN_id4081192.pdf

Casper, K., Ekman, M., & Waedegaard, N. J. (2020). Diplomacy in the digital age: Lessons from Denmark's TechPlomacy initiative. *The Hague Journal of Diplomacy*, 15(2). https://doi.org/10.1163/1871191X-15101094

Casper, K., Ekman, M., & Waedegaard, N. J. (2022). Chapter 12: Diplomacy in the digital age: Lessons from Denmark's TechPlomacy initiative. In *Ministries of Foreign Affairs in the World* (pp. 263–272). https://doi.org/10.1163/9789004505889_013

Cameron, L., Lamers, L., Leicht-Deobald, U., Lutz, C., Meijerink, J., & Möhlmann, M. (2023). [Title]. *AIS Electronic Library (AISeL)*. https://core.ac.uk/download/554503538.pdf

Charter, M., & Clark, T. (2007). [Title]. https://core.ac.uk/download/103312.pdf

Chaturvedi, S., Ladikas, M., Stemerding, D., & Zhao, Y. (2015). [Title]. *Springer Science and Business Media LLC*. https://core.ac.uk/download/42136809.pdf

Cimpeanu, T., Han, T. A., Lenaerts, T., Pereira, L. M., & Santos, F. C. (2022). *Springer Science and Business Media LLC*. https://core.ac.uk/download/492530781.pdf

Clean Clothes Campaign. (2014). *DigitalCommons@ILR*. https://core.ac.uk/download/33619160.pdf

Cohen, J. E. (2006). *Scholarship @ GEORGETOWN LAW*. https://core.ac.uk/download/70374569.pdf

Cornish, H., Fransman, J., & Newman, K. (2017). [Title]. *Christian Aid*. https://core.ac.uk/download/143477120.pdf

Cottey, A., Csernatoni, R., Dobber, J., Fiott, D., Ghalehdar, P., Groitl, G., & Martill, B. (2022). *LSE Ideas*. https://core.ac.uk/download/511316322.pdf

Dahan, M. (2012). [Title]. *Murdoch University*. https://core.ac.uk/download/pdf/12237606.pdf

Daria, F.-F., & Pir-Budagyan, M. (2023). The interplay of technology and international relations: A historical and forward-looking perspective. *Georgetown Journal of International Affairs*. https://doi.org/10.1353/gia.2023.a913637

Dine, J., & Koutsias, M. (2013). [Title]. *Edward Elgar Publishing*. https://core.ac.uk/download/16388018.pdf

D'u43rso, S. C. (2018). *e-Publications@Marquette*. https://core.ac.uk/download/213089166.pdf

Eggeling, K. A. (2023). Digital diplomacy. *Oxford Research Encyclopedia of International Studies*. https://doi.org/10.1093/acrefore/9780190846626.013.790

Elbe, S. (2021). [Title]. *SAGE Publications*. https://core.ac.uk/download/416688432.pdf

Elder, J., Kuhlmann, S., & Smits, R. (2024). [Title]. https://core.ac.uk/download/pdf/6428270.pdf

Egenhofer, C., & Fujiwara, N. (2008). [Title]. https://core.ac.uk/download/5082065.pdf

Ei, A., Sunday O., Lizette N., Ugochi A. A., Jovita I., Amarachi S. E., Eze U. D., Maureen U. A., Brian O. O., Ifeoma B. U., Loveth I. E., Mercy A. N., Nneoma N. O., Ngozi A. O., & Nkeiruka G. O. (2024). Assessment of the learning management systems in tertiary institutions in Nigeria: A narrative review of published studies from 2008 to 2024. *Nursing & Healthcare International Journal*.

Erman, E., Furendal, M., Geith, J., Klamberg, M., Lundgren, M., & Tallberg, J. (2023). [Title]. http://arxiv.org/abs/2305.11528

Falkner, R., & Jaspers, N. (2012). [Title]. *MIT Press - Journals*. https://core.ac.uk/download/223650.pdf

Fantin, S., Ferreira, A., & Pupillo, L. (2020). [Title]. https://core.ac.uk/download/287647893.pdf

Federico, V. (2017). Responsible innovation in developing countries: An enlarged agenda. https://doi.org/10.1007/978-3-319-64834-7_6

Feng, L., & Moodley, K. (2008). [Title]. *Arcom*.

Fritsch, S. (2011). Technology and global affairs. *International Studies Perspectives*, 12(1), 27–45. https://doi.org/10.1111/J.1528-3585.2010.00417.X

Fosca, G., Francesca, P., Giovanni, C., & Salvatore, R. (2021). [Title]. https://core.ac.uk/download/559257952.pdf

Fujii, K. H. (2023). The invitation to constructive exchanges. *Journal of Legislative Studies*, 29(3), 374-391. https://doi.org/10.1080/13572334.2023.2278451

Gersbach, H. (2020). Democratizing tech giants! A roadmap. *Economics of Governance*, 21(4), 351–361. https://doi.org/10.1007/S10101-020-00244-5

Grevi, G. (2020). [Title]. https://core.ac.uk/download/323112026.pdf

Grover, S. A., Williams, C. J., Co-Dyre, A., Malkin, D., Whitlock, J., & ACCESS consortium. (2024). Abstract B069: ACCESS: Advancing childhood cancer experience, science, and survivorship in Canada. *Cancer Research*.

Hall, A., & Kingiri, A. (2024). [Title]. https://core.ac.uk/download/pdf/6480582.pdf

Hall, K., & Regan, M. C. (2016). [Title]. *FLASH: The Fordham Law Archive of Scholarship and History*. https://core.ac.uk/download/144231468.pdf

Hare, P. W. (2019). [Title]. *Springer Science and Business Media LLC*. https://open.bu.edu/bitstream/2144/39129/4/CorrodingConsensusBuilding_AM.pdf

Hagedoorn, J., & Narula, R. (2024). [Title]. https://core.ac.uk/download/pdf/6937130.pdf

Hagedoorn, J., & Narula, R. (2024). [Title]. https://core.ac.uk/download/pdf/6936972.pdf

Harfouche, A., & Nakhle, F. (2023). [Title]. *CREA Forestry and Wood*. https://core.ac.uk/download/553286973.pdf

Heaven, D. (2019). Taking on the tech giants. *New Scientist*, 242(3228), 18–19. https://doi.org/10.1016/S0262-4079(19)30778-X

Hellmeier, M., & von Scherenberg, F. (2023). [Title]. *AIS Electronic Library (AISeL)*. https://core.ac.uk/download/567667291.pdf

Hulvey, R., & Simmons, B. (2023). [Title]. *Penn Carey Law: Legal Scholarship Repository*. https://core.ac.uk/download/572705594.pdf

Huzair, F., & Kale, D. (2011). [Title]. *Innogen*. https://core.ac.uk/download/109590.pdf

Igonor, A., Ikitemur, G., & Karabacak, B. (2020). [Title]. *FUSE (Franklin University Scholarly Exchange)*. https://core.ac.uk/download/386976301.pdf

Irion, K. (2024). [Title]. https://core.ac.uk/download/pdf/6618334.pdf

Ittekkot, V., & Baweja, J. K. (2023). Science, technology and innovation diplomacy in developing countries. *Springer Nature*.

Jan Gunnarsson. (2024). [Title]. https://core.ac.uk/download/pdf/7051611.pdf

Jamshid Kazimi, H., & Harshita Thalwal. (2024). *7th International Conference on Green Technology and Sustainable Development (GTSD)*. https://www.semanticscholar.org/paper/64e35122c519fc2f0404921af98648231c2011a7

Jarrín, M. T., & Riordan, S. (2023). Science diplomacy, cyberdiplomacy and techplomacy in EU-LAC relations. *Springer Nature.*

Jarrín, M. T., & Riordan, S. (2023). Techplomacy. In *United Nations University Series on Regionalism.* https://doi.org/10.1007/978-3-031-36868-4_5

Jess Woodall, K., Klee Aiken, & Tobias Feakin. (2024). [Title]. *Australian Strategic Policy Institute.* https://core.ac.uk/download/pdf/30674827.pdf

J. Verma. (2023). Ethical concerns for the global technological societies: Some observations. *Mind and Society.* https://doi.org/10.56011/mind-mri-122-20231

J. W. McCarthy, M. Visger, & D. A. Wallace. (2019). *DigitalCommons@UM Carey Law.* https://core.ac.uk/download/212819600.pdf

Kariuki Nyaga, J. (2024). [Title]. https://core.ac.uk/download/pdf/6618321.pdf

Kilovaty, I. (2020). [Title]. *UCI Law Scholarly Commons.* https://core.ac.uk/download/328019147.pdf

Klee Aiken. (2024). [Title]. *Australian Strategic Policy Institute.* https://core.ac.uk/download/pdf/30675091.pdf

Koutzias, M. (2020). Digital diplomacy: Conversations on innovation in foreign policy. *LANHAM: Rowman and Littlefield.*

Kvaleberg, O., & Lexau, S. (2024). [Title]. *Saint Louis University.* https://core.ac.uk/download/617933119.pdf

Lunati, M. (2023). [Title]. *ODU Digital Commons.* https://core.ac.uk/download/595866316.pdf

Lungu, S. (2005). [Title]. https://core.ac.uk/download/5076087.pdf

M. Marzouki, & A. Calderaro. (2022). *Internet Diplomacy*. Rowman & Littlefield.

M. R. (2021). *Techplomacy: Innovative Diplomatic Practice or Highest Stage of Neoliberalism in Global Digital Governance?* 2021 IPSA World Congress, International Political Science Association.

Mainwaring, S. (2020). [Title]. *Cambridge University Press (CUP)*. https://core.ac.uk/download/323058085.pdf

Mashiah, I. (2023). Tech-diplomacy: High-tech driven rhetoric to shape national reputation. [Title].

McFarland, J. W. IV. (2022). *Monterey, CA; Naval Postgraduate School*. https://core.ac.uk/download/554153826.pdf

Meryem Marzouki. (2021). Techplomacy: Innovative diplomatic practice or highest stage of neoliberalism in global digital governance? *2021 IPSA World Congress, International Political Science Association*.

Mishago, T. (2012). *GGU Law Digital Commons*. https://core.ac.uk/download/233104379.pdf

Moosavian, S. (2024). Security and technology in the modern global order. *Journal of International Relations*. 2024.

Mustapha, R. A. (2024). *Monterey, CA; Naval Postgraduate School*. https://core.ac.uk/download/618458562.pdf

National Research Council. (2015). Diplomacy for the 21st century. *National Academies Press*.

National Security Commission on Artificial Intelligence (U.S.). (2020). [Title]. https://core.ac.uk/download/482295821.pdf

Naveen Jeyaraman et al. (2024). *Cureus*, 16(8), e67486. https://www.cureus.com/articles/278342-revolutionizing-health care-the-emerging-role-of-quantum-computing-in-enhancing-me dical-technology-and-treatment.pdf

Nizza, V. C. (2024). [Title]. https://core.ac.uk/download/61233 6188.pdf

Orts, E. W. (2001). [Title]. https://core.ac.uk/download/524862 765.pdf

Paton, R., & Spear, R. (2010). [Title]. *The Carnegie UK Trust.* https://core.ac.uk/download/3441.pdf

Pavlina Ittelson & Martin Rauchbauer. (2023). Tech diplomacy practice in the San Francisco Bay Area. *Diplo.*

Rana, K. S. (2004). The 21st century ambassador. *Diplo Foundation.*

Rana, K. S. (2011). 21st-century diplomacy. *Bloomsbury Publishing USA.*

Radanliev, P. (2024). [Title]. *Springer Nature.* https://core.ac.uk /download/598036338.pdf

Renaud, K., & Zimmermann, V. (2019). [Title]. https://core.ac. uk/download/323052064.pdf

Robles Carrillo, M. (2021). [Title]. *Elsevier BV.* https://core.ac. uk/download/479173631.pdf

Robertson, C., & Stein, J. G. (2011). Diplomacy in the digital age: Essays in honour of Ambassador Allan Gotlieb. Toronto: Signal.

Sandoval, M. (2013). *Informa UK Limited.* https://core.ac.uk/d ownload/18295062.pdf

Sandre, A. (2015). Digital diplomacy: Conversations on innovation in foreign policy. Lanham: Rowman & Littlefield.

S. Royo, V., Pina, J., & Garcia-Rayado, J. (2020). Decide Madrid: A critical analysis of an award-winning e-participation initiative. *Sustainability*, 12. https://doi.org/10.3390/su12041674

Sattar, I. (2023). *Monterey, CA; Naval Postgraduate School*. https://core.ac.uk/download/610636840.pdf

Sheryn Lee. (2015). *Australian Strategic Policy Institute*. https://core.ac.uk/download/pdf/30671711.pdf

Singh, I. (2023). The code of connection. *Pencil*.

Stahn, A., & van Hullen, V. (2007). [Title]. https://core.ac.uk/download/5080588.pdf

Stavenes, M. (2020). [Title]. *University of Agder*. https://core.ac.uk/download/351640822.pdf

T. H. Lee, & G. H. Lee. (2000). [Title]. *Springer Science and Business Media LLC*. https://core.ac.uk/download/348124387.pdf

Vander Maelen, C. (2020). [Title]. *Informa UK Limited*. https://core.ac.uk/download/287939745.pdf

Vasen, F. (2017). Responsible innovation in developing countries: An enlarged agenda. https://doi.org/10.1007/978-3-319-64834-7_6

Viviano, J. (2022). [Title]. *ScholarSpace @ JCCC*. https://core.ac.uk/download/523289311.pdf

Watkins, J. D. (1997). Science and technology foreign affairs. *Science*, 227(5326), 650–651. https://dialnet.unirioja.es/servlet/articulo?codigo=427495

Webb, A. (2009). [Title]. https://core.ac.uk/download/81971.pdf

Wilkerson, D. W. (2001). Digital diplomacy. *Bloomsbury Publishing USA*.

Wheeler, G. E. (1969). Civic affairs — How deeply should companies be involved? *Management Decision*, 3(1), 34–36. https://doi.org/10.1108/EB000881

Witt, A. C. (2022). Taming tech giants. *The Antitrust Bulletin*, 67(2), 187–189. https://doi.org/10.1177/0003603x221084153

Zhang, M. (2020). [Title]. *The Ohio State University Libraries*. https://core.ac.uk/download/305123572.pdf

Zhukov, D. (2021). Tech giants versus nation states: Prospects for digital multipolarity. *Journal of International Analytics*, 5(2), 29–44. https://doi.org/10.12737/2587-6295-2021-5-2-29-44

www.ingramcontent.com/pod-product-compliance
Lightning Source LLC
Chambersburg PA
CBHW051537020426
42333CB00016B/1966